Dubai Land Registration No. 2007/05

Property Investment Guide

UAE
Abu Dhabi
Dubai
Sharjah
Ajman
Umm Al Quwain
Ras Al Khaimah
Fujairah

Issue 1 - 2006
Issue 2 - 2008

Copyright © **2008** Cross Border Legal Publishing FZ LLC

ISBN 978-9948-03-581-7

Published by
Cross Border Legal Publishing FZ LLC
Suite 313, Building 8, Dubai Media City
PO Box 502129
Dubai, United Arab Emirates.
Phone: 00971 4 390 3520
Fax: 00971 4 390 8219
info@crossborder.ae
www.crossborder.ae

Printed by
Emirates Printing Press
in the United Arab Emirates

Printing permit
Issued by The Ministry of Information & Culture
No. 3125
June 12, 2006

Disclaimer

The Property Investment Guide is an information resource compiled and updated by Cross Border Legal Publishing FZ LLC based on the latest information available directly from the property developers themselves and financial and legal experts who are shaping the scene. The information in this Guide should not be construed as specific legal or financial advice on individual matters. Every effort is made to ensure the accuracy of the information published herein. However, as the property market in the country is constantly evolving and changing, the publishers cannot be responsible for any changes that are not known before going to print. Keep yourself updated and keep us publishing by supporting the Property Investment Guide on a regular basis.

About this Guide

The winds of change continue to blow over the Emirates. Plan Abu Dhabi 2030 and Dubai Strategic Plan 2015 have both been announced in 2007. Both these plans present a clear picture of the scales of the visions that the Rulers of these Emirates have. Abu Dhabi will be transformed into a sophisticated global city representing the best in culture and quality. The development of the city will have a humane face and will uphold the past as a shining example to the future. The 'Corporation of Dubai' will gallop ahead in its bustling manner and continue to elicit praise for its innovative development. The goal to create a futuristic cosmopolitan city is well underway. All of this bodes very well for the infant property market in the region.

Plan Abu Dhabi 2030

3 Million Residents

7.9 Million Visitors

74,500 Hotel Rooms

686,000 Residential Units

Culture · Transportation · Environment · Public Housing · Social Development · Sustainability

Sheikh Khalifa bin Zayed Al Nahyan

Dubai Strategic Plan 2015

2.5 Million Residents

40 Million Visitors

110,000 Hotel Rooms

650,000 Residential Units

Tourism · Transportation · Construction · Financial Services · Social Development · Infrastructure

Sheikh Mohammed bin Rashid Al Maktoum

In addition, the other emirates of Sharjah, Ajman, Umm Al Quwain, Ras Al Khaimah and Fujairah no longer have a tentative approach towards attracting foreign investment via sale of property. An emirate by emirate description of developments is as follows.

Abu Dhabi has seen some significant developments in architectural style and an increase in demand for premium residential apartments.

The following have been recently announced:

- Ferrari will construct the Ferrari Theme Park on Yas Island
- Warner Brothers will build a theme park in Abu Dhabi
- Frank Gehry is designing the Guggenheim Abu Dhabi, and Zaha Hadid will design the Performing Arts Centre

- The Louvre will come to Abu Dhabi and be designed by Jean Nouvel
- Tadao Ando is designing the Maritime Museum to showcase the capital's maritime history
- The design of the infrastructure of Al Reem Island is nearly complete.

Dubai continues to attract commercial and property investors, with the imminent completion of the Burj Dubai Tower and Business Bay complex. New developments, such as Nakheel's Furjan development, give greater flexibility to investors to tailor their properties to their own requirements.

Some of the property highlights of 2007
- The first villas and shoreline apartments on the Palm Jumeirah were handed over
- The first Jumeirah Beach Residence Units were handed over to residents
- All three phases of Business Bay announced and rapidly sold out
- The revised master plan of the Palm Deira was unveiled
- The QE2 was purchased by Istithmar
- Burj Dubai became the world's tallest free-standing structure, at 150 stories
- Damac launched Signature Residences supported by Ivana Trump
- Dubai World Central Phase 1 construction begun.

Sharjah is a residential alternative to Dubai. Its most notable project, Nujoom islands, is expected to be completed in 2010.

Ajman was the second emirate after Dubai to introduce freehold property in 2004. Currently there are around 11 real estate commercial and residential projects in Ajman.

Ras Al Khaimah was the second emirate in the UAE to permit foreign ownership of property in the UAE and the first to pass a freehold ownership law in November 2005. With the launch of the new media free zone, demand for residential properties has increased in this northern emirate.

Fujairah is the leading beach resort emirate of the UAE, and has residential developments in addition to commercial tourism projects that exploit its beach front.

Developers have exploited the coastal front of **Umm Al Quwain** to introduce waterfront projects, including Umm Al Quwain Marina and White Bay.

Key Trends in the Property Market - 2007

Delays

Not just in delivery of the property but also in the infrastructure. Due diligence continues to be key. Investigation of project completion. Support facilities and infrastructure is critical to ensuring one' property will be realistically ready when one needs it to be.

Market Tests
The practice of select launches targeted at niche markets is being implemented seriously before a developer takes the plunge. The prelaunch is then fine tuned to cater to real needs in the market place.

The Metro
Demand for real estate near the planned Dubai Metro stations is becoming a buzz word and properties command premiums on locations close to these.

Entertainment, Sport and Culture Tourism
From the development of luxury resorts like the Atlantis, to the purchase of the QE2 by Istithmar, Warner Bros signing with Aldar to create a theme park complex, and the already developing vision of Dubailand, entertainment and sport offerings are set to become magnets for tourists. On the other hand, the announcement of the establishment of the Louvre and Guggenheim indicate the beginning of culture tourism.

Inflation
At a record high in the Emirates (Dubai's rate of inflation is suggested at 10%) is making the gold edged dream look a bit brassy. For professionals and employees it has been a gloomy year. Salaries have not kept pace with the increase in expenses.

Better Laws
The announcement of several new laws in Dubai has increased Investor confidence. As everything becomes more complex, more checks and balances are falling into place.

Infrastrucure
At the moment it's a rumour – Roads, Water and Electricity (especially for cooling) are under strain – so watch this space.

Cityscape and other Property Exhibitions
Cityscape has become an unavoidable attendance opportunity to update oneself on emerging business in property. The industry gets a huge networking and awareness boost at the event. Serious professionals are only available at the event on most days.

Research
Numbers are becoming increasingly important. With new data emerging all the time, predictions based on these are sought after. We have featured EFG Hermes' views based on as accurate a collection of data as is possible,

Hidden Costs
Maintenance charges, other annual charges, and Gymnasium costs are the guises that these

costs come in. The Housing Tax charged on a monthly basis by the municipality can represent a hefty outgoing as well on large investments.

Home Owners Associations

An important organization for owners to communicate with developers. 2007 has witnessed a lot more systematic methods for the implementation of these.

Rising Construction Costs

Real estate professionals and contractors are in demand and the price of materials is on the up.

Skewed demand and supply

Large family villas are the residence of choice but are in short supply. Apartments for people requiring basic space in a good location are seriously needed, but the market place is awash with luxury apartments replete with expensive leisure facilities and little other infrastructure. Investors may want to consider buying a property that is not iconic but is likely to address the needs of the majority of the working population.

> The Property Investment Guide (UAE) is essentially a collection of viewpoints from the country's Property Industry. We have chosen editorial from a wide selection of contributors and hopefully the reader will be able to arrive at an informed decision.

Developers Section

There are the Master Developers who are putting together projects that involve billions of Dirhams of investment and will house tens of thousands of people, and there are niche developers. A summary of the developers featured in this publication, is as follows:

Master Developers

Aldar - Yas Island, Al Raha Beach Development and Central Market Redevelopment

Sorouh - Shams Abu Dhabi, Saraya and The Golf Gardens

Reem Developers - Najmat Abu Dhabi and Rawdhat Abu Dhabi

EMAAR - Arabian Ranches, Downtown Burj Dubai, Emirates Living, Dubai Marina an Umm Al Quwain Marina. Iconic buildings like the Burj Dubai – the tallest building in the world and the Armani Hotel are but two of their individual offerings.

Nakheel - Palm Jumeirah, The World, Palm Jebel Ali (PJA) and Dubai Waterfront (DWF), Palm Deira, Discovery Gardens, International City, Jumeirah Park, Jumeirah Village

Dubai Properties - Jumeirah Beach Residence, Business Bay, Culture Village, Bay Square, Al Waha Villas and The Villa

Union Properties - MotorCity, UPTOWN Mirdiff, Green Community and Green Community West, Iconic buildings like Index and Limestone House

Tameer Holdings - Al Salam City and a series of luxury high rises and other properties

SNASCO - Al Basateen, Sharjah Investment Centre
RAK Properties - Julfar Towers, Mina Al Arab
Al Hamra Real Estate - Al Hamra Village
Mina Al Fajer – Coastline development in Fujairah including Mina Al Fajer Resort
Besides these large scale projects, the same developers and numerous others have boutique and niche projects. These would form an unending list as the reader can gauge by seeing the list of developers featured at the end of the section. We have featured the following developers whose offerings begin to describe the variety of the developments.

ETA STAR - Goldcrest Dreams, The Summit, Starhill Towers & Gallery
KM Properties – The Tamani range of properties
ACI Properties – Dubai Star, Q Sami Tower, Victory Bay
Al Fara'a Properties – The Manhattan, Le Grand Chateaux
Khoie Properties – La Hoya Bay and future developments in La Hoya Bay
Ishraqah – Seasons Community and The Onyx
Schön Properties – Dubai Lagoon

It should be mentioned here as well that the following developers and their developments are worth studying. We have been unable to feature them in this guide.

Tatweer - Dubailand
SAMA Dubai - The Lagoons
Dubai World Central - Dubai Civil Aviation
Nujoom Islands - Artificial Islands in Sharjah

Real Estate Agents and Secondary Market Section

Possibly the area that, in the property market, has seen the largest growth of companies is the real estate agency segment. The prospective tenant, landlord, developer has to make choices of exclusive and non exclusive access to a real estate agent. While agencies with highly established credentials may be able to negotiate and tie up a deal better, business can come from anywhere at all, so justifying exclusive deals is becoming increasingly difficult. Having said that, there are innumerable costs and documents to be considered regarding property on the rental and secondary market. These vary almost from developer to developer and should be scrutinized with great detail.

We have featured **LLJ** - specialists in the Abu Dhabi market, **Better Homes** – the most established agency in the Emirates and beyond – with research and experienced agents. **Engel & Völkers** and **Dubai Luxury Homes** are representative of quality agencies with databases and access to potential buyers overseas. **Eqarat.com** represents the online broker – the internet is the most useful starting point. Besides these, the listings at the end should give testimony to the fact that this is a booming market.

Finance

EFG - Hermes has provided us with defnitive research and analysis of the Property Market.

Mortgages are now an offering from so many banks, it is easier to qualify for a mortgage than even a year ago and customers have ample choice even in Islamic Finance.

Global Eye sums up the mortgage situation by giving practical advice.

We have featured **Dubai Islamic Bank** and its Islamic Finance package, **Barclays Bank** – that is becoming 'your friendly mortgage adviser' with its consumer friendly branding.

The **Comparative Mortgage Chart** features most other banks and their schemes.

Real estate funds have begun to make an appearance and though we have not featured any yet, there is no doubt that confidence remains.

Legal Advice

The legal situation pertaining to property seems to be heading towards stability. Dubai continues to lead the way in setting precedents.

Lisa Dale from **Al Tamimi & Company** gives a brief overview of the laws in all the Emirates.

Jimmy Houala, managing partner of **Bin Shabib & Associates** updates us on all the new laws that have been announced and analyses them as well.

Helene Mathieu Consultants advises on the Escrow Law that has created the most ripples and truly tempered the market for the better.

Inheritance for expatriates – an issue that has not been evaluated as this issue has not become an urgent one in this infant market is dealt with by **Alexis Waller and Catherine Gill** from **Clyde & Co**.

Useful Websites

www.uaeinteract.com
www.abudhabi.ae
www.dubai.ae

www.cityscape.ae
www.dubailand.gov.ae

Research is available at
www.oxfordbusinessgroup.com
www.gulfnews.com
www.futuregroup.ae
www.colliers.com
www.bhomes.com

The UAE

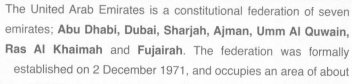

UAE and Dubai

The United Arab Emirates is a constitutional federation of seven emirates; **Abu Dhabi, Dubai, Sharjah, Ajman, Umm Al Quwain, Ras Al Khaimah** and **Fujairah**. The federation was formally established on 2 December 1971, and occupies an area of about 83,000 sq km along the south-eastern tip of the Arabian Peninsula. Qatar lies to the west, Saudi Arabia to the south and west, and Oman to the north and east. **The capital and the largest city of the federation, Abu Dhabi**, is located in the emirate of the same name.

Four-fifths of the UAE is desert, but it is also a country of contrasting landscapes, from awe-inspiring dunes to quaint oases and stunning mountains to fertile plains. As one of the world's fastest growing tourist destinations, it boasts sun, sand, sea, sports, shopping, top-class hotels and restaurants, an intriguing traditional culture, and a safe and welcoming environment. The **UAE's business capital is Dubai**, while **Sharjah city is the cultural capital**.

The UAE was estimated to have 4.32 million residents in 2004. Approximately 80% of the population comprises expatriates from all over the Arab world, Asia, Europe, Africa and America.

Key Indicators

Population 4.32 million (2004)

Area 82,880 sq km

Major language Arabic (Business is conducted in English)

Major religion Islam

Life expectancy 76 years (men), 81 years (women)

Monetary unit 1 Dirham (AED) = 100 fils (pegged to the dollar at AED 3.68=1USD)

Main exports Natural Gas, Crude Oil

GDP USD 103 billion (2004 in Current prices)

GDP growth rate 7.4% (2004)

Export of goods and services USD 82.58 billion (2004)

Foreign Direct Investment USD 483.2 million

Source: www.uaeinteract.com

History

Prior to independence, the UAE was known as Trucial Oman, (also known as the Trucial States), and the component sheikhdoms of the territory were under British protection. In 1892, the sheikhdoms´ defence and external relations were governed by the United Kingdom, although they were otherwise autonomous and followed the traditional form of Arab monarchy, with each ruler having absolute power over his people.

Petroleum, the basis of the area's prosperity, was first discovered in 1958, when deposits were located beneath the coastal waters of Abu Dhabi.

Before the discovery of oil in Abu Dhabi, economic activity in the seven emirates was dominated by pearling and fishing, which were the primary source of employment of the population, together with agriculture and handicrafts. Although there was a long history of trade in the UAE, overseas trade was limited during the domination of the British colonial powers. The discovery of onshore petroleum in Abu Dhabi in 1960 heralded the beginning of increased revenue for the state. Commercial exploitation of petroleum began in 1962, and in January 1968 the United Kingdom announced its intention of withdrawing the British military forces from the area by 1971. In March 1968 the Trucial States joined nearby Bahrain and Qatar (which were also under British protection) in what was named the Federation of Arab Emirates.

The interests of Bahrain and Qatar proved to be incompatible with those of the smaller sheikhdoms and choosing to separate from the Federation in August 1971 they became separate independent states. In July of that year, six of the States (Abu Dhabi, Dubai, Sharjah, Umm Al Quwain, Ajman and Fujairah) agreed on a Federal Constitution for achieving independence as the United Arab Emirates. The UK terminated its special treaty relationship with the States, and the UAE became independent on 2 December 1971.

The late Sheikh Zayed bin Sultan Al Nahyan, ruler of Abu Dhabi and president of the UAE at its inception, was quick to seize on the potential of the oil industry. He accelerated the development of the emirates by reinvesting oil revenues back into healthcare, education and the national infrastructure. The oil industry resulted in an influx of expatriate workers and residents who now make up more than three quarters of the population. His son, Sheikh Khalifa bin Zayed Al Nahyan is the current ruler of the UAE.

The country's growing business sector and its tourism industry have helped to fuel a construction boom. Billions of dollars are being invested into residential and commercial development projects. Today, the UAE is one of the most liberal countries in the Gulf, comprising a diverse population and tolerating other cultures and beliefs.

Source: United Arab Emirates General Information Authority

Commercial Milestones

1959 Dnata (Dubai National Travel Agency) is established.

1963 The National Bank of Dubai is established.

1968 National Bank of Abu Dhabi is established as the Central Bank until the Currency Board is founded in 1975.

1971 Dubai Islamic Bank is formed, the first full-service Islamic bank in the world. The United Arab Emirates is formed with six member states.

1972 UAE joins the International Monetary Fund. Ras Al Khaimah joins the United Arab Emirates.

1976 Abu Dhabi National Oil Company is established, the first government-owned company to specialise in the marketing and distribution of petroleum products in the country.

1979 Etisalat, the UAE telecommunications services corporation, is established. Ras Al Khaimah Bank (RAK Bank) is established.

1980 Sheikh Rashid bin Saeed Al Maktoum signs a decree establishing Jebel Ali Free Zone (Jafza), Dubai's business hub and free zone.

1982 Damac Holdings is established, providing a multitude of services including property development, education and hospitality.

1985 Emirates Airline is launched, which is now one of the leading airlines in the world.

1990 UAE's GDP is AED 125,300 million.

1994 Cabsat is launched, and is now an annual showcase for telecommunications, media and technology.

1996 Sharjah Airport International Free Zone is established.

1997 Emaar Properties is formed and listed on the Dubai Financial Market. It is now a market leader in property development in the UAE and internationally.

1999 Burj Al Arab hotel, reaching 321 metres, is declared open. It has become a major tourist attraction in Dubai.

2000 Dubai Internet City (DIC) Free Zone is launched as the Middle East's largest IT infrastructure.

2001 GDP of the UAE is AED 221,751 million. Dubai Media City (DMC) Free Zone is launched and is home to global media businesses.

2003 GDP is AED 241,828 million.The Dubailand project, twice the size of Disney World Florida, is launched.

2005 Dubai International Financial Exchange is launched in September, creating the first international exchange in the UAE. DP World, the corporate integration of Dubai Ports Authority and DPI Terminals, becomes one of the largest global port operators to date.

2007 Burj Dubai - located in the newly created 'Downtown Dubai' becomes the tallest man made structure in the world.

Economic Landscape

The UAE has no income tax, no corporate tax and no other significant taxes. Government expenditures as a share of GDP increased 4.3 percentage points to 36.9 percent in 2001, compared to a 4 percentage point decrease in 2000. The Economist Intelligence Unit (EIU) reported that the UAE government consumed 17 percent of GDP in 2001. In the same year, based on data from the EIU, the United Arab Emirates received 58.83 percent of its total revenues from public enterprises in the hydrocarbon sector. Data from the International Monetary Fund's 2003 World Economic Outlook indicates that from 1993 to 2002, the UAE's weighted average annual rate of inflation was 2.51 percent.

The UAE economy is now ranked as the second largest economy in the Arab region, its GDP amounting to USD 181 billion in 2007, up from USD 163 billion in 2006. This is outweighed only by Saudi Arabia. Dubai is the second richest emirate after Abu Dhabi. Although it had modest oil reserves, the emirate has used its resources wisely, and today 90% of Dubai's GDP is non-oil based.

Foreign Investment
Foreign investment in the UAE is restricted. Recent developments have resulted in foreigners having the right to own property and businesses in specially designated 'investment' areas. All businesses (apart from free zone entities) must be at least 51% owned by a UAE national. Foreign investment is restricted in the banking, telecommunications, and petroleum sectors. There are no controls or requirements on current transfers, access to foreign exchange, or repatriation of profits. Foreign ownership of land and stock is also restricted.

Banking and Finance
There are 21 domestic banks, 14 of which have some federal or local government ownership, and 26 foreign banks in the UAE. The majority of projects are government backed, making them a secure and attractive proposition for international investment banks.

The UAE has no corporate income tax, but there is a 20 percent tax on foreign bank profits. The World Trade Organisation requires that the UAE should end the current restriction on allowing new foreign banks into the country, so the number of foreign banks is likely to increase.

Banks are restricted to lending only up to 7 percent of their capital to any single foreign institution, and up to 25 percent of bank funds in commercial bonds or shares. Non-residents are prohibited from owning over 20 percent of the shares in UAE national banks.

Currency
The unit of currency in the UAE is the Dirham (AED or Dhs), made up of 100 fils. The

Dirham is linked to the US dollar at a rate of USD1 = AED 3.68. The numerous local and international banks offer all of the usual banking services with some offering offshore banking. There are no government restrictions on the international transfer of funds into or out of the country. There is no tax levied on income in the UAE. However, new residents are advised to check their own country's taxation policy in the event that they may have to pay taxes in their own countries.

Property Ownership

 At this point foreigners can own property in designated areas in a few emirates. These are conditional and of various types. The UAE Federal Law currently is ambiguous about 'Freehold ownership' by expatriates. Resident visas can be issued to property owners. The number of visas issued may depend on the size of the investment.

In August 2005, a law was issued by H. H. Sheikh Khalifa bin Zayed Al Nahyan, President of the UAE and Ruler of Abu Dhabi, granting differing rights of land ownership to UAE nationals, GCC citizens and other expatriates in the emirate of Abu Dhabi. The law grants GCC citizens the right to own land in designated Investment Areas. The other emirates are predicted to follow with similar laws.

Cost of Living

The cost of living varies from emirate to emirate, but in Abu Dhabi and Dubai it is comparable to other large cities around the world. Below is a breakdown of typical costs in Dubai - per person.

Water AED 50 / month

Electricity AED 300 - 600 / month (for an apartment)

Telephone (rates per minute on a land line)

Within an emirate calls are free. Inter emirate call charges vary, max AED 0.24

USA: AED 2.12 (peak) / AED1.37 (off peak)

UK: AED 2.69 (peak) / AED 1.91 (off peak)

Australia: AED 2.69 (peak) /AED1.91 (off peak)

India: AED 2.40 (peak) AED1.98 (off peak)

Saudi Arabia: AED 2.12 (peak) AED 1.37 (off peak)

Petrol AED 6.75 per gallon (Super)

Groceries for a family of 2 AED 500 / week

Restaurants

Fast food meal for 2 adults: AED 50

Meal at an informal restaurant for 2 adults: AED 200

Buffet meals (offered at many 5 star hotels): AED 170 / person

Hairdressers

Female: AED 150

Male: AED 50

Cultural Landscape

Religion

Much of the UAE reflects a tolerant and relaxed society, respecting other religions but with its origins and roots in Islam. There are Christian churches in Dubai, as well as Hindu and Sikh temples. Dress and diet are predominantly dictated by religion, but Dubai reflects a more cosmopolitan lifestyle.

Ramadan is the ninth month of the Muslim calendar. During this month Muslims observe the Fast of Ramadan, which lasts for the entire month during the daylight hours. During Ramadan most restaurants are closed during the daylight hours. After sunset, the fast is broken with a meal known as Iftar. Residents and visitors respect the holy month of Ramadan by not consuming food or drink in public places in the UAE. Ramadan ends with the festival of Eid al Fitr, one of the two most important celebrations in the Islamic calendar.

Language

- Arabic is the official language of the UAE, although English is widely spoken and understood, and is considered the business language.
- Road signs in Dubai and throughout the UAE are in both Arabic and English, and telephone automation systems allow you to choose between the two languages.

Weather and Climate

- Moderate climate is found between October and March, when the days are sunny and the nights are much cooler (average temperature range from a high of 26 degrees C to a low of 15 degrees C).
- Summer is between April and September, with temperatures peaking at 50 degrees C, high humidity levels and occasional sand storms.
- The UAE has a sub-tropical, arid climate. Sunny, blue skies can be expected most of the year. Rainfall is infrequent and irregular, falling mainly in winter. Temperatures range from a low of about 10.5 degrees C, to a high of 48 degrees C.

Alcohol

- Alcoholic beverages are available in all licensed bars and restaurants in hotels and nightclubs in some of the emirates, including Dubai and Abu Dhabi.
- An Alcohol Licence is required by non-Muslims earning at least AED 3,500 per month, to purchase alcohol from licensed shops for home consumption.
- There is a zero drink driving tolerance rule in the UAE, and alcohol is not permitted for consumption in Sharjah.

Recreation

The emirate of Dubai in particular is a popular tourism magnet. There are amusement and water parks for families and, for the more adventurous, desert driving, camping, hiking, rock climbing and diving. Developed beaches coupled with a 'service friendly' environment are some of the factors that enhance tourism. Cinemas show the latest international films; and concerts, plays and exhibitions take place throughout the year. Private clubs offer facilities for activities ranging from golf to swimming to gymnasium. The Northern Emirates are also popular for all the natural beauty of the Hajar Mountains and the sea.

Across the Emirates

Ski Dubai

 Located in Dubai's Mall of the Emirates, Ski Dubai is the first indoor ski resort in the Middle East and offers indoor skiing, snowboarding and tobogganing. Ski Dubai is a unique mountain-themed attraction that offers the chance for visitors to experience real snow in the middle of the desert all year round, and encompasses 5 ski runs that vary in difficulty, height and steepness; the longest run being 400 metres with a fall of over 60 metres. Private and group lessons are available by appointment.

Qasr al-Hosn

Located on Khalid bin Walid Street, the White Fort or Old Fort is the oldest building in Abu Dhabi. The original structure was constructed in 1793 as the official residence of Abu Dhabi's rulers, and major renovations took place in 1983. Admission is free.

Heritage Village/Bedouin Village

 Located behind the Abu Dhabi International Exhibition Centre on Mussafah Road, this heritage village has an authentic replica of a bedouin encampment prior to the impact of oil wealth on the emirate. An elaborate mud-brick house and a traditional mosque, traditional souq, and camel riding can be experienced, and visitors can watch a demonstration of the age-old sport of falconry. Admission is free.

Al Ain Oasis

This is an extensive date plantation in the centre of town near Al Ain Museum and is an attractive tourist spot. The plantation is divided into small date farms, with permanent access for farmers' vehicles and for pedestrians. Two small mosques are situated within the palm groves. Admission is free.

Dreamland Aqua Park

Dreamland is located in Umm Al Quwain, and has 29 water rides, numerous water attractions and a variety of restaurants.

Shooting Club, Umm Al Quwain

A superb venue for fans of this sport. Activities include laser shooting simulator, shooting real weapons inside or outside, and pistol, skeet and trap shooting. The Club also has a restaurant, bar and live music.

Dubai Museum

The Al Fahidi Fort located in Bur Dubai behind Al Fahidi Street, houses Dubai Museum. The old fort building contains regular exhibits of weapons, traditional costumes and musical instruments and the courtyard has good examples of huts and wooden boats. The new underground section of the museum houses lifelike exhibits of an ancient souq, a Quran school, typical Arabic households and an oasis. There is also a display on the desert by night with interesting local wildlife. A separate room is dedicated to lively modern exhibits of pearl diving and fishing.

Burj Al Arab Hotel

Designed to resemble a billowing sail, the hotel is 321 metres tall. This all-suite hotel is considered one of the finest hotels in the world.

Sheikh Saeed Al Maktoum House

Located on the southern bank at the entrance to the Creek in Dubai, the house was the residence of the ruling family in the 1800s. The traditional coral-block structure has four wind towers and a large central courtyard, carved teak wood doors, wooden lattice screens and balustrades.

Heritage and Diving Village

Located next to Sheikh Saeed Al Maktoum House in Al Shindagha in Dubai, the village features

reconstructions of Dubai's maritime past. Attractions include a tented bedouin village with traditional weapons, chests and household utensils. Gift shops sell handicrafts. Folk dance and music performances are staged from time to time. There are a number of cafeterias and a seafood restaurant in the Shindagha village.

The Arabian Wildlife Centre, Sharjah

The Arabian Wildlife Centre is the only 'zoo' in Arabia that has all the animals native to the Arabian Peninsula. Opened in September 1999, this excellent facility houses over 100 species displayed in safe, spacious and natural surroundings. The centre displays the diversity of the fauna and raises awareness of the species that have and are becoming extinct.

Le Meridien Al Aqah Beach Resort, Fujairah

Located between the Hajar Mountains and the Indian Ocean on a superb stretch of Al Aqah Beach in the emirate of Fujairah, the resort is on the east coast of the United Arab Emirates, approximately 15 kms from Dibba Village, 49 kms from Fujairah town and 90 minutes from cosmopolitan Dubai. Activities include a professional diving centre with easy access to many east coast dive sites, watersports centre (windsurfing, sailing, water-skiing), three tennis courts, children's recreation area with pool and 230 metres of white sandy beach.

Jebel Hafeet

Jebel Hafeet is a mountain primarily in the United Arab Emirates on the outskirts of Al Ain. The mountain actually straddles part of the border with Oman. The mountain rises 1240 metres and offers an impressive view. Jebel Hafeet was a well-known landmark throughout the area's history and is a contemporary tourist attraction. A splendid winding road leads to the top.

Wadi Bih

A spectacular traditional route from the west coast through the Hajar mountains to the east coast, Wadi Bih is a scenic drive not to be missed. Driving through narrow gorges with isolated stone huts, the natural beauty of this drive is unique.

The Seven Emirates

Abu Dhabi

Abu Dhabi, by far the largest emirate, is ruled by the Al Nahyan family. It occupies 67,340 sq km or 86.7% of the total area of the country. The emirate is primarily a vast desert area with about two dozen islands in the coastal waters, including the island where the city of Abu Dhabi is located, plus six sizeable islands further out in the Arabian Gulf. The population of the emirate is concentrated in three areas: the capital city, Abu Dhabi; Al Ain, an oasis city located near the Hajar Mountains; and the villages of the Liwa oases. Traditionally, the population along the coast relied on fishing and pearling for their livelihood, whilst those in the hinterland relied on date plantations and camel herding. This is fast changing as Abu Dhabi strives to put its oil income to good use by investing in development (the Guggenheim, Louvre and Warner Brothers are already setting up branches here) that will present the emirate in a cultured and sophisticated light. H.H. Sheikh Khalifa bin Zayed Al Nahyan is the current ruler of Abu Dhabi and the president of the UAE.

Dubai

Dubai, the second largest of the seven emirates, is ruled by the Al Maktoum family. It occupies an area of approximately 3,900 sq km, which includes a small enclave called Hatta, situated close to Oman, amongst the Hajar Mountains. Dubai, the capital city is located along the creek, a natural harbour, which traditionally provided the basis of the trading industry. Pearling and fishing were the main sources of income for the people of Dubai. Under the wise leadership of its rulers, Dubai's focus on trade and industry transformed it into the leading trading port along the southern Gulf. H.H. Sheikh Mohammed bin Rashid Al Maktoum is the current ruler of Dubai, and the Vice President and Prime Minister of the UAE. Dubai is known for its five star nightlife, a myriad of restaurants, shopping festivals and the constant ability to surprise and inspire.

Sharjah

Sharjah, which shares its southern border with Dubai, is ruled by the Al Qasimi family. It is approximately 2,600 sq km and is the only emirate to have coastlines on both the Arabian Gulf and the Gulf of Oman. In the nineteenth century the town of Sharjah was the leading port in the lower Gulf. Produce from the interior of Oman, India and Persia arrived here. Sharjah's salt mines meant that salt constituted an important part of its export business, along with pearls. In the 1930s when the pearling industry declined and trade decreased due to the creek silting up, Imperial Airways' flying boats set up a staging post for flights en route to India, which benefited the residents of Sharjah. Today, under the leadership of H.H. Sheikh Sultan bin Mohammed Al Qasimi, Sharjah is the cultural and educational centre of the UAE and takes pride in preserving the country's cultural heritage as well as promoting Arab culture and traditions.

Ajman

Ajman is the smallest emirate, comprising only 260 sq km. It is ruled by the Al Nuaimi family. Surrounded mostly by the emirate of Sharjah, Ajman also possesses the small enclaves of Manama and Musfut in the Hajar Mountains. Along the creek, dhow building was the specialised trade. Fishing and date-trees provided the local population with their primary means of sustenance. Ajman benefited greatly from the union of the emirates, a fact that is reflected today in their stately buildings and infrastructure. H.H. Sheikh Humaid bin Rashid Al Nuami has ruled since 1981.

Umm Al Quwain

Umm Al Quwain is ruled by the Al Mualla family. It is the second smallest emirate, with a total area of around 770 sq km. Positioned between the emirates of Sharjah and Ajman to the south and Ras Al Khaimah to the north, Umm Al Quwain has the smallest population. Fishing is the local population's primary means of income. Date farming also plays a significant role in the economy. After the union of the emirates in 1971 Umm Al Quwain developed into a modern state, and continues to progress under its present ruler, H.H. Sheikh Rashid bin Ahmed Al Mualla.

Ras Al Khaimah

Ras Al Khaimah, the most northerly emirate, is ruled by another branch of the Al Qasimi family. It covers an area of 1,700 sq km. Thanks to the run-off water from the Hajar Mountains, Ras Al Khaimah has a unique abundance of flora, so it is no surprise that agriculture is important to the local economy. The emirate also benefits from its stone quarries, and fishing, which is plentiful in the rich waters of the Gulf. The city of Ras Al Khaimah, situated on an inlet, has a rich history. It was renowned for its prosperous port and for its exquisite pearls, which were famous as being the whitest and roundest available anywhere. Ras Al Khaimah's current ruler is H.H. Sheikh Saqr bin Mohammed Al Qasimi.

Fujairah

The only emirate without a coastline on the Arabian Gulf is Fujairah, which is ruled by the Al Sharqi family. Situated along the coast of the Gulf of Oman, Fujairah covers about 1,300 sq km. Unlike other emirates, where the desert forms a large part of the terrain, mountains and plains are its predominant features. Fujairah's economy is based on fishing and agriculture. Like Ras Al Khaimah, the land in Fujairah is irrigated by rainwater from the Hajar Mountains, making it ideal for farming. H.H. Sheikh Hamad bin Mohammed Al Sharqi is the present ruler.

Developers

A view of the island of Abu Dhabi

Heralding the age of the super-developers in the region, **ALDAR Properties PJSC** is spearheading the infrastructural progress of the UAE as the top real estate development, management and investment company. Headquartered in Abu Dhabi, its vision is to establish the federal capital as the UAE's most dynamic forward-thinking real estate market by creating unique and prestigious developments that can be considered a benchmark of quality.

ALDAR'S portfolio was initially focused on Abu Dhabi, but has now recently expanded its remit with projects in North Africa. Characterised by comprehensive planning, innovation and a commitment to excellence in urban design, town planning and sustainable development, ALDAR believes in balancing the evolving needs of a modern city with maintaining and conserving the environment. Therefore its projects seek to prioritise both the immediate and future physical, social and economic requirements of the UAE and Abu Dhabi for the benefit of those who live and work in the region.

With a key competitive advantage due to its sound financial backing, large resources, high level of management expertise and government support in undertaking large-scale, market-driven projects which add value to the emirate's booming property industry, ALDAR's competitive edge is undisputed.

Yas Island, Abu Dhabi

The dynamics of change in Abu Dhabi are such that it is difficult to stand back from the day-to-day rhythm of existence and gain a clear overview of the innovative model of integrated leisure development coming into existence. Many world firsts are attached to the development of Abu Dhabi's Yas Island, the region's latest mega theme park and leisure destination.

Yas Island, one of Abu Dhabi's larger islands, is roughly one third the size of the island of Abu Dhabi, and features a beachfront shoreline approximately 32 km long. Infrastructure is being developed around the Yas Island project in advance and to the operational benefit of the capital city. A new 10-lane highway will soon connect Yas Island to Abu Dhabi International Airport, the Abu Dhabi - Dubai highway, and the city of Abu Dhabi at Mina Port. Yas Island will also connect to ALDAR Properties' signature Al Raha Beach development with Lagoon hotels, marinas, polo clubs, apartments, villas, a golf course and food and beverage outlets aplenty, Yas Island is repositioned as a unique international tourist destination.

With construction that started in early 2007, Yas Island extends over a total land area of 2,500 hectares (25 million sq m), of which 1,700 hectares (17 million sq m), will be claimed for

Ferrari Theme Park – Yas Island

development. Attractions such as the world-class Formula 1™ (F1) motorsport race track, signature hotels, the Ferrari Theme Park, marinas, a water park, the Warner Brothers Park and a mall development with a 300,000 sq m retail area are the core elements being developed to cater to the needs of a rapidly expanding population and an inbound tourism sector that is voracious for novelty, choice and an integrated leisure lifestyle.

Located on the island will be four major marinas, a Ferrari Theme Park and yachting facilities; resort hotels, lagoon hotels and hotel apartments; a water theme park, one links golf course, a polo field and equestrian centre; restaurants and cafes, and mixed-type residences. Plans are also underway to adapt sensitive and beautiful parts of the island into conservation areas.

Developed by ALDAR, Abu Dhabi's leading developer, the park is expected to transform the island into a USD 45 billion world-class, mixed-use destination with tourist attractions including beaches, entertainment, shopping, hotels, residences, golfing, equestrian facilities and motor racing. 'Yas Island will combine the many natural attractions of an island with the world's most popular leisure activities,' said ALDAR chairman Ahmed Ali Al Sayegh. 'We have taken people's passion for the sea, for racing cars, shopping, golfing and luxurious living, and designed them all into a single unique setting. Yas Island will be the only destination in the world that combines our desert and maritime traditions with the fascination of Florida and the elegance of Monte Carlo. It will be the world's most complete leisure destination and also host the world's first Ferrari Theme Park.'

The Ferrari Theme Park is a branded entertainment destination offering a range of 24 themed attractions to appeal to people of all ages. A 65 metre-high 'G Force Tower' is set to be a high-thrill ride with a motor racing theme. As a world first, this twin rollercoaster ride allows two people to race. The development will also offer an 18-screen theatre complex and a wide range of food and beverage outlets.

Among the core attractions is the **Formula 1™ Grand Prix track**. The F1 tie-in with the development is a monumental step in the world of motor racing, with the landmark announcement that one of the world's F1 races will be held on the island in 2009. Ferrari, as a brand synonymous with F1 racing, has placed its name behind this multi-billion dollar development which is part of the UAE government's vision to further place Abu Dhabi on the world stage. The project has been trusted to ALDAR Properties to oversee its construction and total management, as the world's most comprehensive multi-leisure destination.

Already under construction, the 2009 Formula 1™ Abu Dhabi Grand Prix track was designed by renowned Formula 1™ circuit designer Hermann Tilke in consultation with ALDAR. The motorsport race track will be one of the longest and most demanding tracks in the world and will include an iconic grandstand and hairpin bend for the ultimate in spectator entertainment. This premium F1 race track will wind its way around villages, marinas and sand dunes. Visitors will

Located on the island will be 4 marinas and yachting facilities, resort hotels, lagoon hotels and hotel apartments, a water park, one golf course, a polo field and equestrian centre, restaurants and cafes, and mixed residences. Plans are also underway to adapt sensitive parts of the island into conservation areas.

be able to enjoy viewing the race track from the sky deck of the ALDAR signature hotel or from the comfort of a super-yacht berthed in the marina. Better still, the circuit can be test-driven by amateurs and visitors to the island, accompanied by seasoned instructors as part of the only Ferrari driving school in the world outside of the famous Ferrari Maranello base.

His Highness Sheikh Mohammed bin Zayed Al Nahyan said, 'A Formula 1™ Grand Prix is one of the world's most prestigious sporting events, in the same category as the Olympic Games or World Cup, and is unrivalled in terms of continuous global resonance. That is why this new partnership is such an exciting one for Abu Dhabi and the entire UAE.'

Formula 1™ Management CEO Bernie Ecclestone commented, 'We are delighted to welcome Abu Dhabi into the Formula 1™ family, and look forward to a long and successful partnership. Abu Dhabi's hospitality, the genuine warmth of its people, and an ever-increasing number of world class facilities, will ensure that its round of the FIA Formula 1™ World Championship is a wonderful addition to the Formula 1™ calendar.'

Development of the Ferrari Theme Park and associated residential and commercial areas will be undertaken in two phases, with completion due in 2014.

ALDAR CEO Ronald Stephen Barrott elaborated on Yas Island, and its mission for success,"Our intention is to bring together families, friends and individuals seeking options of entertainment, excitement, nature and peace in one location".

What else does Yas Island include?

Retail
The retail centre on Yas Island will consist of an area of 300,000 sq m built over three levels and will offer a truly unique shopping experience. A central exhibition arena will offer the ideal venue for fashion shows, concerts and product launches. Well-known anchor stores will allow shopaholics to choose from a variety of exclusive brands. The retail centre will also incorporate a kid's zone, fitness centre, video arcades and a bowling alley, as well as four hotels and even a dedicated ladies spa providing beauty and health services.

Hotels and Beach Resorts
Yas Island will be dotted with diverse golf, marina, lagoon and beach hotels and resorts that will offer a unique world of choice for residents and visitors.

Water Park
Yas Island's water theme park will offer something for everyone. The Giant Maelstrom, Velkoma Water Bomber, Master Blaster and the enclosed three metre Hurricane Rides will appeal to all

Al Dana at Al Raha Beach

Al Bandar at Al Raha Beach

thrill-seekers. The water park will offer activities such as the Family Boomerang and the Bubba Tub ride, an activity pool with a giant 'Rain Fortress', wave pool and a lazy river to entertain the family. Other highlights will include cable waterskiing, scuba diving and a beach. Kids will also enjoy access to an exclusive children's pool with slides.

Leisure and Sport

Guests of Yas Island will be able to engage in a multitude of action sports and leisure-based activities whilst visiting. In addition to the Ferrari driving experience, Yas Island will offer a polo field and equestrian centre as well as a golf course, while a full range of watersport activities will keep even the most active member of the family entertained.

Residential

Yas Island will offer a variety of modern low-rise, mixed-use residential apartments and villas to rent, lease or own. The architecture will be a blend of the traditional with the modern. Guests will be able to choose from a range of waterfront apartments or terraced stand-alone units with panoramic views of the golf course, or opt for the two-tiered exclusive waterfront apartments by the lagoons.

For further info go to www.yasisland.ae

Al Raha Beach Development, Abu Dhabi

As a mega-billion Dirham project set to house a staggering 120,000 residents, Al Raha Beach is ALDAR's signature development and will be built along 10 km of natural beachfront overlooking the Arabian Gulf. This project will offer a unique, unparalleled lifestyle through its world-class facilities for residential, commercial and public use on the outskirts of Abu Dhabi towards Dubai.

The development consists of eleven precincts each with its own distinct character and appeal. The Al Raha Beach Development takes inspiration from great waterfront cities of the world to maximise Abu Dhabi's natural wealth of water and stunning beachfront. Set to be the Gulf's most spectacular new address, Al Raha Beach is destined to become a world-class waterfront community and a major visitor attraction for Abu Dhabi.

Careful planning and attention to detail is what will make Al Raha Beach prominent amid other development projects in the UAE. Its infrastructure has been designed to allow free-flowing vehicle and foot traffic throughout the city. This is a part of the project about which ALDAR Chief Executive Officer, Ronald Stephen Barrott is passionate: 'Accessibility has been a very important factor in the design of Al Raha Beach. A light rail system, along with jet cats and water taxis are planned for the project to ensure that all residents have easy access to their properties, and that commuting into Abu Dhabi or Dubai will be easy and accessible.'

Central Market   www.aldar.com

The introduction of the water taxi service, serving all parts of Abu Dhabi Island as well as outlying islands such as Sadiyat and the international airport, is also set to provide a new form of urban transport for the city and add another dimension to tourism for the emirate. Residents will be able to enjoy stunning waterfront views from their homes, with the total development set to appeal to anyone who enjoys marine sports. This ideal living and working environment will ensure that the attraction of Al Raha Beach will appeal far beyond Abu Dhabi residents and will attract foreign investors in search of a truly unique lifestyle experience.

For further info go to www.alrahabeach.ae

Central Market Redevelopment, Abu Dhabi

The Central Market project is a prestigious and fully integrated, mixed-use redevelopment in the heart of downtown Abu Dhabi, updating on a grand scale the former market area. The new Central Market will be a centrepiece for Abu Dhabi as well as ALDAR Properties, which has been awarded an exclusive concession by the Government of Abu Dhabi to redevelop the 45,000 sq m site.

At the heart of the redevelopment will be the transformation of the existing Central Market area into a vibrant new town centre. For over forty years it was the centre of trade and a focal point for citizens and tourists to purchase supplies and explore, or simply a meeting point to while away time. The iconic development will keep this rich history alive with a traditional souk, combined with the modern features of a luxury shopping complex, a large choice of high quality restaurants, savvy apartments, two hotels and state-of-the-art office accommodation all within a tastefully landscaped environment, marking Central Market on the map as a new place to shop, work and live. For more information on Central Market, please visit www.centralmarket.ae

ALDAR Properties PJSC
P.O. Box 51133
Abu Dhabi
United Arab Emirates

Tel: +971 2 6964444
Fax: +971 2 6417501
E-Mail: info@aldar.com
Website: www.aldar.com

Shams Abu Dhabi

Abu Dhabi based **Sorouh Real Estate** was established on June 26, 2005 with a commitment to promote a spirit of innovation. This spirit led the company to develop a vision that sets it apart from competitors and meets the needs of residents and workers in today's urban developments.

Sorouh's corporate vision is to "bring communities to life in perfect balance". Its real estate projects utilize innovative design, state-of-the-art technology and the latest in construction techniques designed to meet the four core needs of human wellbeing: physical, intellectual, social and spiritual. The comprehensive approach to building communities that offer balanced lives requires new planning approaches and design skills both of which are secured amongst the staff and through partnerships with world renowned experts. Some of the world's best architects and engineers have joined forces with Sorouh to create inspiring yet practical living spaces that truly bring life in perfect balance.

This spirit of innovation is evident in all projects from Shams Abu Dhabi, the flagship development on Reem Island, to the Golf Gardens, the capital's first residential Golf course development.

Projects

Sorouh now has around AED 40 billion worth of projects under development. These include:

Shams Abu Dhabi on Reem Island, a landmark development within Abu Dhabi and the UAE. Close to the city yet offering a lush green island setting, Shams Abu Dhabi will be a unique urban location, a self-contained community and will offer 60,000 residents a perfect combination of modern comfort and natural living.

The Central Park of Shams Abu Dhabi, with its extensive recreational and educational offerings, will become a favoured destination for residents of both Reem Island and the city of Abu Dhabi. With its broad expanses of green and exceptional edutainment, retail and relaxation amenities, the Central Park will undoubtedly take its place in the pantheon of great city parks.

The Gate District is a cluster of 8 towers located at the entrance to Shams Abu Dhabi. Now architecturally renowned worldwide the AED 11 billion residential, office and retail development is designed as a gateway to the peninsula from Reem Island. The Gate District also includes the 74 storey Sky Tower which will be a pinnacle of luxury for its residential and commercial occupants when completed.

The Central Park of Shams Abu Dhabi

The Golf Gardens Abu Dhabi

The Golf Gardens will be the first commercial venture in Abu Dhabi to combine golf and real estate. With its beautiful villas and townhouses overlooking the golf course, this development will raise the bar for residential property in Abu Dhabi.

Also under development is **Tala Tower** which overlooks the Marina in Reem Island, giving panoramic views of the Abu Dhabi skyline. It offers waterside living just five minutes from the heart of the city.

Also extending along Abu Dhabi's prestigious Corniche is **Saraya**, a location that offers panoramic views and encompasses high class residential complexes with new age leisure facilities as well as modern commercial trade units.

Sorouh is also developing the **Abu Dhabi Aviation Authority residential project,** and in its first venture outside the UAE, Sorouh will also be involved in developing the 7,000,000 sq ft **Bab Al-Bahr** project in Morocco.

Sorouh Real Estate
PO Box 93666
Abu Dhabi, United Arab Emirates

Tel: +971 2 4440006
Fax: +971 2 4440066
Website: www.sorouh.com

ريـــم للتطويـــر

REEM DEVELOPERS

Unlocking the Potential of Real Estate

Bay Centre - Najmat Abu Dhabi on Reem Island

Reem Developers was launched in May 2006 as the fully-owned subsidiary of Reem Investments, an Abu Dhabi-based private joint stock company, with a paid-up capital of AED 1.555 billion.

The company is one of the region's leading companies that focus on a holistic approach to real estate developments, covering master plan design, construction, and management. It defines lifestyle standards and determines regional architectural and urban planning trends. It remains committed to its business philosophy and principles of providing ample opportunities for property developers and offering quality services to its valued investors. This philosophy coupled with a comprehensive management approach has enabled Reem Developers to make its mark in the industry.

Reem Investments is continuing to shore up the company's assets globally through prudent investment of financial and human resources in three sectors – financial, industrial and real estate – in the UAE, the region and around the world.

Reem Developers has firmly established itself as a leading player in the Abu Dhabi real estate market by successfully launching two high-profile projects, Najmat Abu Dhabi and Rawdhat Abu Dhabi.

Work on both projects has been progressing as per schedule and the company is planning an aggressive expansion programme through the acquisition of prime real estate assets globally, with a distinct immediate focus on North Africa and India. Several of its deals in these countries are in an advanced stage, the details of which will be announced shortly.

Reem Developers has also been successful in inducting some of the finest professionals into its team and retaining their services. Many renowned architects, engineering consultants and project managers have been working on its projects to ensure its developments meet the highest international standards in terms of planning, management and execution.

Najmat Abu Dhabi

Najmat – the Star of Abu Dhabi – is the flagship project of Reem Developers, which is expected to further boost Abu Dhabi's global appeal. It envisages development of 16 million square feet of prime seafront area on Al Reem Island. The island, which is barely 300 metres off the coast of Abu Dhabi's city centre, was recently declared an International Investment Zone.

Grand Canal - Najmat Abu Dhabi

Maysan at Najmat Abu Dhabi

There are many factors that make Najmat one of the best waterfront developments in the region. It occupies the prime seafront of Reem Island. Marina, canal and water features are all designed to ensure that all residents enjoy the waterfront. In addition, the buildings are also graded in heights to offer all residents an unobstructed view of the sea. Environmental concerns are addressed through water flushing and safeguards for marine life.

Najmat Abu Dhabi, which has been conceived as a mixed-use project, blends traditional and contemporary architecture to showcase an idyllic island lifestyle. This project has been meticulously and aesthetically master-planned by renowned international architects, town planners and designers. Investors are presented an exciting range of waterfront plot options ranging from office and residential to hospitality and retail.

Najmat Abu Dhabi's marina emerges as a business and entertainment hub, as it is a centerpiece of one of the largest and most exclusive shopping malls in the region.

The mall has two signature towers that redefine the city's skyline. They have a mix of office, retail and residential space. The marina will also feature two five-star hotels with boardwalks and ample berthing space in addition to waterfront shops, cafes, restaurants and public art galleries. Open green areas, walkways and trails offer residents ample opportunities for recreation. A team of international experts will provide environmental safety guidelines to protect the marine life, flora and fauna.

Maysan at Najmat Abu Dhabi

Maysan, the Residential District, at Najmat Abu Dhabi – signifies sophisticated lifestyle and is tempered by the generous open spaces and community facilities. One of its outstanding features will be a variety of water movement 'experiences' that will be featured throughout the development. These will include generous waterside promenades, cascading water features, fountains and open parklands to complement the built areas.

It is a premium all-residential neighborhood that comprises mid and high-rise towers spread over approximately 2,000,000 sq ft. It has been conceived as an environmentally conscious 'total community experience,' drawing inspiration from some of the most outstanding developments of its kind worldwide. Maysan is located close to the heart of Najmat Abu Dhabi's Central Business District.

Rawdhat - Abu Dhabi

Rawdhat Abu Dhabi is being planned as a dedicated 'develop to lease' community with a master-plan to attract the discerning professionals. Its privileged residents will be able to enjoy a total lifestyle with amenities for leisure activity and luxurious living.

This project with its advanced and sophisticated urban planning approach will become a place that embraces contemporary lifestyles and celebrates the vibrancy of life in itself. It is an urban village that nurtures communal and sustainable living in an atmosphere of opulence, comfort and tranquility. The development capitalizes on the inherent character of the site within the context of Abu Dhabi – the capital of the United Arab Emirates. The urban spatial language encourages the sense of place and belonging by carefully considering all aspects involved – infrastructure and management, layout and clustering, circulations and accesses, open spaces and community facilities, and building heights and styles.

Rawdhat Abu Dhabi will showcase themed residences on 61 plots. These will range from low to mid-rise residential towers with all modern amenities. This will have a backdrop of lush green landscape with parks, scenic trails and walkways.

Construction work on this landmark project, which is completely sold-out, is progressing as per schedule.

Reem Developers
Abu Dhabi Trade Centre, Abu Dhabi Mall
East Tower, 4th Floor
P.O. Box 37646
Abu Dhabi, United Arab Emirates

Tel: +971 2 6444455
Fax: +971 2 6444463
Email: info@reemi.ae
Website: www.reemdevelopers.com

Emaar Properties PJSC is one of the world's largest real estate companies and is rapidly evolving to become a global provider of premier lifestyles. A Dubai-based Public Joint Stock Company, Emaar is listed on the Dubai Financial Market and is part of the Dow Jones Arabia Titans Index. Emaar has highlighted the remarkable global growth of the company by debuting on the Financial Times Global 500 ranking, which provides an annual snapshot of the world's largest companies.

In tandem with Dubai's rapid growth, Emaar has been shaping landscapes and lives in the emirate since the company's inception in 1997. Not just building homes, Emaar develops value-added, master-planned communities that meet the homebuyers' full spectrum of lifestyle needs. A pioneer of innovative community-living concepts, Emaar is the prime mover of the emirate's real estate and construction sector.

With **six business segments** and more than **60 active companies**, Emaar has a collective presence in over **36 markets spanning the Middle East, North Africa, Pan-Asia, Europe and North America**. The company has established operations in the **United Arab Emirates, Saudi Arabia, Syria, Jordan, Lebanon, Egypt, Morocco, Algeria, Libya, India, Pakistan, Turkey, Indonesia, USA, Canada** and the **United Kingdom**.

Emaar's international projects include: **Marassi**, an upmarket tourism resort; **Uptown Cairo**, a master-planned residential project; a residential community in New Cairo City; and **Cairo-Alexandria Desert Road Community project**, a mixed-use development - all in Egypt; **Boulder Hills**, a world-class leisure and residential community in Hyderabad; **Mohali Hills** in Punjab and **The Palm Springs** in Gurgaon, India; multiple resort projects in Morocco, including **Amelkis II & III, Bahia Bay, Oukaimeden, Saphira and Tinja** - luxury residential golfing communities; **Samarah Dead Sea Golf & Beach Resort** in Jordan; **Eighth Gate project** in Damascus, the city's first master-planned community; **Highlands** and **Canyon Views** in Islamabad, and **Crescent Bay** in Karachi, Pakistan; **Tuscan Valley** in Istanbul; and a **residential and leisure project in Lombok Island**, Indonesia.

An artist's rendering of Downtown Burj Dubai

On the following pages are featured several Emaar projects in different stages of completion across the UAE.

Downtown Burj Dubai

Downtown Burj Dubai is Emaar's flagship project and will be a mixed-use 500-acre community combining commercial, residential, hotel, entertainment, shopping and leisure outlets in open green spaces dotted with lakes and other water features.

Located at its centre is Burj Dubai, which will offer premium residential and retail space. It will be surrounded by The Old Town, The Old Town Island, The Dubai Mall, Burj Dubai Square, Burj Views, Burj Dubai Boulevard, The Residences, restaurants, hotels, residential facilities and more - all located on the banks of a spectacular lake.

The development will drive Dubai's premier downtown. Apart from the signature architecture of the Burj Dubai and The Dubai Mall, what makes it special is its proximity to Sheikh Zayed Road and Dubai's main commercial centres.

The development will be self-sustaining with a 24-hour lifestyle and a buzz that percolates right through the residential, retail, business, entertainment, leisure and dining facilities. It will be the place to live, work and play.

Downtown Burj Dubai Components

Burj Dubai
The iconic signature tower, the tallest in the world, due for completion in 2008, will be the centrepiece of Downtown Burj Dubai.

The Dubai Mall
The Dubai Mall is a 5.8 million sq ft shopper's paradise with 3.77 million sq ft of leaseable retail space.

The Old Town
The Old Town development ranges from low-rise three storey apartment buildings to exclusive mid-rise towers with penthouses. Architectural cues are taken from traditional Arab style terraces, balconies, recesses and niches make for comfortable outdoor living.

Al Manzil and Qamardeen Hotels, The Old Town
Four-star deluxe hotels operated by the South African Hotel chain Southern Sun.

The Old Town Island
A low-rise development, The Old Town Island has four quarters – Al Bahar, Tajer, Attareen and The Palace Hotel, Old Town.

The Palace Hotel, Old Town
Located on The Old Town Island.

Burj Dubai - the tallest building in the world rising above the city of Dubai

Set near The Montgomerie Dubai Golf Course, Emirates Hills represents luxury beyond compare.

Burj Dubai Square

Burj Dubai Square is the perfect choice for businesses in Dubai, with over 1 million sq ft of prime office space.

The Burj Dubai Boulevard

Inspired by great boulevards of the world it will provide a thoroughfare through the Downtown Burj Dubai community.

The Lofts

Located on the Boulevard, The Lofts is a six-storey podium with private garden courts and air-conditioned shopping arcades.

Boulevard Walk

Located in close proximity to the Burj Dubai Boulevard it features studio to two-bedroom apartments along with retail shops located on the ground floor.

South Ridge

A six-tower cluster of stylish residential apartments.

Burj Views

Three residential towers plus podium near Burj Dubai Boulevard, The Dubai Mall and Old Town.

Burj Dubai Lake Hotel and Serviced Apartments

A 63-storey property with fully equipped service apartments.

The Residences

One of the first residential communities at Downtown Burj Dubai with nine high-rise residential apartments.

Armani Hotel

Located in the Burj Dubai, includes 160 guest rooms and suites, restaurants and a spa covering more than 40,000 sq m.

Emirates Living

Emirates Living is a lifestyle concept from Emaar that encompasses some of its key master-planned residential communities including Emirates Hills, The Lakes, The Greens, The Meadows, The Springs and The Views.

A collection of neighbourhoods, Emirates Living embodies Emaar's commitment to delivering luxurious homes set in tranquil surroundings offering residents all amenities including community centres, retail outlets, health and fitness centres and schools.

Emirates Hills

The first project unveiled by Emaar Properties in 1999, Emirates Hills is a world class development overlooking the lush green fairways of The Montgomerie, Dubai, an 18-hole championship golf course. The course was created by master architect Desmond Muirhead and seven-time European Order of Merit winner, Colin Montgomerie. A golfer's paradise, Emirates Hills features a harmonious balance of well-appointed villas, handsome private neighbourhoods and lush landscaping, making it the most desirable residential community in an inimitable setting.

A property in Emirates Hills with The Montgomerie, Dubai golf course in the foreground.

The Lakes

Emirates Hills comprises Dyaar Al Hambra, the Montgomerie Villas and Maisonettes and Signature Villas.

Dyaar Al Hambra is a collection of luxurious villas that are influenced by traditional Arabian style architecture and incorporating contemporary innovations. The villas feature grand entrance halls and formal entertaining areas; superbly appointed living and dining areas; master bedrooms; spacious family rooms; guest quarters; modern kitchens and bathrooms and broad balconies. The lifestyle element is enhanced by an internal courtyard and complemented by a well-appointed Majlis.

The Montgomerie Villas and Maisonettes are nestled comfortably within the exclusive and private Emirates Hills community. These homes have been designed by international architects and designers, incorporating a touch of Arabian influence. All the villas are tastefully designed and built with attention to detail and super quality of construction, with private gardens.

- Project Type: Plot sales and ready-made villas
- 24 hour professional security
- Pedestrian walkways
- Al Hambra Villas range in plot size from 8,112 sq ft to 9,818 sq ft
- Montgomerie Villas and Maisonettes range in plot size from 2,159 sq ft to 4,119 sq ft

The Montgomerie, Dubai

The focal point of Emirates Hills, an exclusive residential community developed by Emaar, The Montgomerie, Dubai is today one of the Middle East's most luxurious golfing destinations.

The Montgomerie, Dubai's championship golf course was designed by Colin Montgomerie, one of the world's leading golfers, in association with Desmond Muirhead, renowned golf course architect. The course covers 265 acres, which consist of 123 acres of turf, 49 acres of man-made lakes (a total of 14 lakes), 93 acres of landscaped gardens and is scattered with 81 large bunkers.

The Lakes

Tranquil and scenic with waterways, parks and landscaped greenery, The Lakes set the tone for family living in Dubai. Featuring family homes of two to five bedrooms, the project has a community centre, bicycle pathways and 24-hour security and maintenance. The villas are situated between The Montgomerie, Dubai, and the Emirates Golf Course.

- Project type: Detached villas and town homes
- Size: 1,733 sq ft to 3,057 sq ft
- Unit types: three to four bedrooms and single family villas

The Greens, Dubai

The Meadows, Dubai

The Springs, Dubai

- Landscaped community areas with parks, tennis and squash courts, gymnasium and children's play areas
- Interconnected sidewalk system that links residents to community amenities
- The Lakes has five phases – Deema, Furat, Maeen and Zulal, which were completed earlier; and the recently launched Rayaan

The Greens

A mid-rise residential complex, The Greens blends affordability with a new lifestyle choice. Combining tasteful design and fitted with the latest in modern conveniences, The Greens is designed to meet the needs of the family.

Each complex features four individual buildings clustered together to creative an exclusive courtyard environment for the residents. Launched in June 2002, The Greens comprises 36 buildings set over 65 acres. The complex has 3,500 residential units and 4 office buildings.

- Project Type: Mid-rise residential buildings
- Unit type: Studios, one, two, three, and four-bedroom apartments
- Sizes: 372 sq ft to 2,100 sq ft
- State-of-the-art building security
- Secure underground parking

The Meadows

Tranquil and verdant, The Meadows is Emaar's master-planned community featuring tree-lined streets and spacious, distinctive villas. The two-storey homes range from three to seven-bedrooms and have elegant finishes with ceramic tiles and marble stairs. The living areas have 9 ft high ceilings and the fitted kitchens have designer cabinetry. The spacious bedrooms have built-in wardrobes. The Meadows has over 1,800 villas, which come in 20 different architectural styles.

Residential amenities include parks and water features, membership opportunities to The Montgomerie, Dubai and Health Club; swimming pools, children's play area, shopping centres, cafes and restaurants, and 24-hour security and maintenance.

- Project type: Single family detached villas
- Sizes: 3,089 sq ft to 6,419 sq ft
- Unit types: three to seven bedrooms
- Easy access to Dubai Internet City, Dubai Media City and Knowledge Village
- Proximity to The Montgomerie, Dubai and Emirates Golf Club

The Springs

The Springs is a gated community of townhouses with scenic waterways and lush landscaping

The Views, Dubai

making for a perfect residential environment. The Springs is located in close proximity to Dubai Media City and Dubai Internet City, and offers community amenities such as access to shopping centres, community fitness centres and recreational facilities. The single family detached villas come in four floor plans.

The Springs has over 4,800 homes built around scenic lakes. The villas incorporate the finest architectural styles and picturesque landscaping.

- Project type: Single family detached villas
- Sizes: 1,647 sq ft to 5,960 sq ft
- Unit types: two to four bedroom
- 24-hour security and maintenance
- Access to schools and retail facilities

The Views

Emaar Properties highlights its modern community living in The Views, an exclusive community with lakeside apartments that also open to the green vistas of Emirates Golf Club.

At The Views, exquisite Riviera-style mid-rise apartment towers are arranged amid landscaped gardens. Featuring an exclusive courtyard for residents, The Views accentuates its community lifestyle feel through amenities such as a swimming pool, gymnasium, mini-sports court, play areas, retail outlets and parks with walkways.

The Views 'In-Suite' apartments are designed to quality standards and feature open living areas, modern appliances and the latest in technology highlighted by Smart Home Living. The 'Designer Suite' apartments feature stone countertops, quality cabinetry and tiled floor finishes. Assigned parking lots, 24-hour security and card-controlled access for vehicles and pedestrians add to the quality of living.

The Views comprise Lakeside towers including Arno, Travo, Turia and Una; and Golfside towers – Golf Towers, The Fairways and The Links. Mosela and Tanaro offer waterside and golf course views.

- Project Type: Mid-rise residential buildings
- Unit type: Studios, one, two, three and four-bedroom apartments
- Waterside and golf course views
- Fully equipped gymnasium
- Underground car parking
- Children's play areas
- Children's wading pool

An artist's rendering of Dubai Marina

A view of Dubai Marina

- Green parks and walking tracks
- Mini sports courts
- Community shopping centre
- Landscaped pool decks

Dubai Marina

Offering Riviera-style living in a sophisticated environment, Dubai Marina by Emaar Properties is one of the largest waterfront developments of its kind in the region. With a total development area of 50 million sq ft, Dubai Marina encompasses a large canal with 3.5 km of waterfront offering access to the sea from both ends. Frilling the canal are waterfront living apartments.

Dubai Marina comprises ten districts each developed as a distinct community. Several residential towers, hotels, shopping centres and leisure amenities complement the Marina experience that is highly sought after in Dubai. Dubai Marina Walk, which lines the waterfront, has a selection of cosmopolitan restaurants while the boardwalk serves as a link between the many towers in the development, the gardens and the Marina.

Emaar has unveiled six developments at Dubai Marina – Al Majara, Al Sahab, Dubai Marina Towers, Marina Promenade, Marina Quays and Park Island. Three of them – Al Majara, Al Sahab and the Dubai Marina Towers – have been completed and the keys handed over to buyers.

Dubai Marina prepares you to explore the Arabian Gulf. With calm waterways, Dubai Marina will have five Marinas with clean, modern berths that can handle over 500 vessels including powerboats of 20 ft to 100 ft and sailing boats of 30 ft length. The East Marina Stage One with 120 berths and East Marina Stage Two with 60 berths have been completed. Yacht Club Marina with 135 berths, West Marina with 115 berths and Marina Mall with 60 berths will be completed towards the end of this year.

- Project value: USD 4.36 billion
- Construction started: 2000
- Completion date: 2010-2012
- Estimated total population: 75,000
- Total area: 50 million sq ft
- Total developmental area: 3.5 km
- Ten districts, each developed as a distinct community
- Total marine frontage: 11 km
- Mooring facility for 550 vessels

Phase 1
- Dubai Marina's first phase comprises six multi-storeyed towers.

The Marina Promenade

The Dubai Marina Yacht Club

- Three of Emaar's towers are named after precious stones – Murjan, Al Mass and Fairooz.
- The others derive their names from Arab fragrances – Mesk, Yass and Anbar.
- Al Majara is a five-building residence comprising high-rise waterfront apartments overlooking the largest bay of Dubai Marina. Units are one and two bedroom suites of size 744 sq ft to 1,166 sq ft.
- Al Sahab comprises of twin towers, one with 23 floors, the other with 44, offering unparalleled views of the Arabian Gulf. Units are waterfront residential suites. They face the widest part of the Marina's bay.
- Dubai Marina Towers comprises six towers – the 37-storeyed Murjan and Mesk; 28-storeyed Al Mass; 20-storyed Fairooz; 24-storeyed Yass and 16-storeyed Anbar. Units are residential suites.

Under construction
- Marina Promenade comprises six condominium luxury high-rise towers featuring one, two and three bedroom suites. The towers overlook the widest bay of Dubai Marina.
- Marina Quays extends 20 metres over the water assuring an unsurpassed living experience. Marina Quays has a range of retail outlets too. The Marina front towers and homes are completed in three phases – Quay East, West and North – comprising suites and one, two and three-bedroom apartments.
- Park Island has a one-of-a-kind design with the towers so placed to feature parks and landscaped gardens. The marina front towers and homes comprise suites completed in four phases – Blakely, Bonaire, Fairfield and Sanibel.

Dubai Marina Yacht Club
The Dubai Marina Yacht Clubhouse offers an array of marina-related services to members. The elegant clubhouse will feature restaurants, a marine retail shopping arcade, international yacht sale and brokers offices, ships chandlery and nautical gifts store, yachting fashion boutique, charter office and boating school. Membership will be open to boat owners and other patrons.

A modern boat repair facility will feature 50-tonne travel lift with 2 to 3-tonne jib cranes, wash down bay, drainage and settlement tanks, floating work berths, spray paint sheds and administration offices. Services offered include boat lifting and launching, wash down, antifouling, spray painting, boat building, fibre glass repairs, engine repairs, marine electrical repairs and marine fabrication and rigging.

Shopping and Dining facilities
Dubai Marina has extensive retail facilities and a selection of eateries. The Marina Walk, expanding over 60,000 sq ft, offers an exciting tenant mix of quality food and beverage and retail outlets.

A wide range of restaurants caters for every taste. Culinary options include American, Thai,

Umm Al Quwain Marina

Mediterranean, Indian, Japanese, Chinese, Lebanese, and traditional Arabian, apart from several cafes that open to the sea. The retail spread includes supermarkets, book shops and pharmacies.

Other facilities

- Facilities at Dubai Marina include children's play areas, swimming pools, resort spas, games room, lounge facilities, sheltered parking, multi-purpose lounge.
- Access to Dubai Marina Yacht Club with several exclusive benefits for members.
- Easy access to Dubai Internet City, Dubai Media City, Jebel Ali Free Zone, Knowledge Village and Emaar Business Park.
- Nuran Al Majara at Dubai Marina is Emaar's first fully-serviced residence under the brand name Nuran.

Umm Al Quwain Marina

Umm Al Quwain Marina is an AED 12 billion (USD 3.3 billion) development by Umm Al Quwain Marina LLC, the joint venture between the government of Umm Al Quwain and Emaar Middle East. An emerging tourism destination in the UAE, the emirate of Umm Al Quwain is a historic site that sees renewed growth in all sectors of its economy including real estate, industries and banking.

Umm Al Quwain Marina will be a waterfront community along the shores of Khor Al Beidah, Umm Al Quwain's natural lagoon. The project incorporates residential, retail and recreational facilities, sport and yacht clubs, waterfront resorts, boutique hotels, schools, community centres, open beaches, and landscapes with parks and trails.

Umm Al Quwain Marina will cover a land area of about 2,000 acres with 23 km of waterfront. The total navigable water area, including marina and a set of canals, is about 450 acres.

The masterplan envisages 6,000 villas and 2,000 townhouses. Exclusive villas will have facilities to allow owners to moor their boats by their door. A central Town Centre will have retail and leisure facilities; other amenities include indoor gyms, tennis courts and swimming pools. An additional 1,200 resort and hotel-rooms are also planned.

The first and second phase of residences in the Mistral community within Umm Al Quwain Marina has been launched. It comprises a series of Spanish and Portuguese-styled villas.

Umm Al Quwain Marina will have six distinct zones namely: Town Centre Marina Zone; West Mainland Villa Zone; Mainland Townhouse Zone; East Mainland Villa Zone; Three Islands Villa Zone; and Exclusive Island Villa Zone.

A Villa view of the Umm Al Quwain Marina

All clusters will be held together by open spaces dotted with lakes. The landscaping offers pedestrian access to waterfront community recreation centres, retail centres and other amenities.

- AED 12 billion (USD 3.3 billion) development
- Developed by Umm Al Quwain Marina LLC, the joint venture between the government of Umm Al Quwain and Emaar Middle East
- Easily accessible from Dubai through Emirates Ring Road
- An expansive waterfront development spread over 2,000 acres
- 23 km of waterfront
- 450 acres of navigable water area
- Residential, retail and leisure facilities
- Town Centre to have retail and leisure amenities
- Private mooring facility for boats
- Central marina basin of 450 m diameter to berth over 600 boats
- Hotels, waterfront resorts, schools and community centres
- Six zones in masterplan
- Total 6,000 villas and 2,000 townhouses

Emaar Contact Center
UAE (Toll Free) 800-Emaar (800-36227)
Tel: +971 4 3661688
Fax +971 4 3661600
Email: customercare@emaar.ae

NAKHEEL

The Coastline of Dubai in 2002

The Palm Jebel Ali

Dubai Waterfront

The Palm Jumeirah

One of the world's largest privately held real estate developers, **Nakheel** is a key player in realising the vision of Dubai for the 21st century: creating a world class destination for business and tourism.

The vision of Nakheel is rooted in the values and leadership of the late H.H Sheikh Rashid bin Saeed Al Maktoum, who fifty years ago looked upon the blank canvas of the desert and saw a great city rising, and his son, H.H Sheikh Mohammed bin Rashid Al Maktoum, who is bringing this vision to fruition.

A key part of that vision was diversifying Dubai's economy; growing the Emirate into a leading tourism destination. Dubai was already well known for its year-round sun and pristine beaches, but the Dubai coastline was limited to only 70km. It was thus in the late 1990s that H.H Sheikh Mohammed bin Rashid Al Maktoum came up with the ingenious solution of building a man-made island to create more beachfront.

An artist's rendering showing the future shape of Dubai, once Nakheel's landmark projects are completed.

The World

The Palm Deira

Marina Residences - an artist's rendering

Shoreline Apartments

The Villas on Palm Jumeirah

Thus in 2001, The Palm Jumeirah was launched. Measuring 5 km by 5 km, the concept seemed outlandish to many, overly ambitious or even impossible. Yet Dubai and Nakheel's success has been built on saying yes when others say no.

Nakheel now has portfolio of projects ranging across 2 billion square feet of land worth more than USD 30 billion. Already Nakheel has achieved more than many companies achieve in a lifetime. The end of 2006 saw the first residents move onto Nakheel's signature project, and 2007 saw the handover of the first phase of The Palm Jumeirah's 4,000 apartments and villas.

Dubai is the fastest growing city in the world, and Nakheel is a key player in realising the vision of the city for the 21st century, creating a world-class destination for business and tourism.

Nakheel's portfolio now extends to 14 developments: from iconic landmarks that will go down in history for their unprecedented magnitude and grandeur to dream-like residences that redefine community living. Nakheel has already completed several of its projects including The Gardens – a beautifully landscaped 220 hectare residential development in Jebel Ali – and Ibn Battuta Mall. Inspired by the travels of the 14th century explorer Ibn Battuta, the mall features more than 275 retail outlets and 50 entirely new brands.

The Palm Trilogy

The Palm is an extraordinary project of grand proportions – the creation of the world's three largest man-made islands known as The Palm Jumeirah, The Palm Jebel Ali and The Palm Deira. Located just off the coast of Dubai, the three palm tree shaped islands will increase Dubai's shoreline by a staggering 520 km and create a large number of residential, leisure and entertainment opportunities, all within a unique and inspiring setting. Upon completion, the three islands will range across an area larger than Manhattan.

The Palm Jumeirah

Nakheel's signature development, The Palm Jumeirah saw its first residents move in, with 4,000 units being handed over in 2007. This is just the first of many more milestones on The Palm Jumeirah, which will be established as not only one of the region's, but also one of the world's leading tourist destinations.

The first of more than thirty hotels and resorts to open, in November 2008, will be the 1,500 room Atlantis-The Palm, while the 61 storey Trump International Hotel & Tower on The Trunk is destined to become the Dubai skyline's next iconic landmark. Other world renowned tourist attractions on The Palm Jumeirah will be the cruiseliner the QE2, and the spectacular Cirque de Soleil; permanently based at The Palm Jumeirah, 2010 will see the premier of an entirely original Cirque de Soleil specifically created for The Palm Jumeirah.

The Palm, Jumeirah measures approximately 5 km in length and 5 km in width and will be a retreat, a quiet, serene and safe haven for living, leisure and relaxation. There are approximately

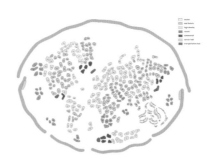

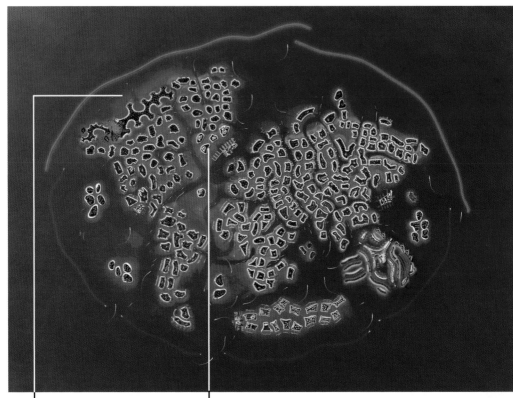

Coral Reef Island Resort - artist's rendering

North America and Greenland

An artist's view of The World by night

7,000 apartments and 1,800 villas and townhouses on The Palm Jumeirah.

The Trunk of The Palm Jumeirah will offer an outstanding array of retail and lifestyle options for residents and tourists to enjoy, creating a new centre for Dubai. The Golden Mile will feature 220 outlets, offering the world's most exclusive brands and an array of boutiques, shops, restaurants and cafes.

The Crescent will feature international hotels of the highest quality, providing the ultimate holiday destination. Located near The Crescent will be a number of fascinating dive sites, and at the head of the Crescent will be Atlantis-The Palm, one of approximately 30 hotels that will appear on The Palm Jumeirah.

The World, Dubai

Realising the vision of H.H Sheikh Mohammed bin Rashid Al Maktoum, Ruler of Dubai and Vice President and Prime Minister of the UAE, Nakheel is creating the most exclusive property development ever, The World.

Four kilometres off the coast of Dubai, The World is an icon in the making. A collection of 300 private and resort islands that are sold by invitation only, the shape of the earth's continents is now visible, with reclamation of The World development on schedule for completion in 2008. Measuring approximately 9km by 7km, The World has evolved into one of the most desirable and exclusive addresses on the planet. The first resorts are due to welcome visitors by the end of 2010.

With The Palm, Nakheel put Dubai on The Map. Now with The World, Nakheel puts the map on Dubai. The World consists of 300 islands strategically positioned to form the shape of the world map, lying 4 km off the coast of Dubai. The World will be the most exclusive and sought after community offering the most exciting residential and leisure opportunities in the fastest growing tourist destination on the planet. This is the ultimate destination where the only limit is your imagination.

Almost two years of extensive planning, research, development and design took place before The World was announced to an astonished real estate industry. Measuring approximately 9 km in width by 7 km in length, the development will cover approximately 9,340,000 sq m, will be visible to the naked eye from space and will add an additional 232 km of beachfront to Dubai's coastline. For The World to take shape, Nakheel is moving over 326 million cubic metres of sand to form the islands and the 26 km long oval shaped breakwater.

This is arguably the most exciting, innovative and visually stimulating real estate development ever. In a land of modern city and timeless desert, old world charm and new world comfort,

Dubai Waterfront

Dubai Waterfront Company, launched early this year, is the largest waterfront offering in the world, occupying the last remaining coastal waterfront of the emirate. The 81 million sq m beachfront will be a mixed-use destination encompassing over 250 master-planned communities and offerings.

Madinat Al Arab is the first phase and focal point of Dubai Waterfront, which has been carefully crafted and developed by an international consortium of the world's best architects, planners and urban developers. Occupying the majority of seafacing land in Dubai Waterfront and designed to be the downtown and central business district, Madinat Al Arab will be anchored by Al Burj, one of the world's tallest buildings that will spiral towards the sky, forming a centrepiece that embodies the ambition, vision and magnitude of the development.

Heavily influenced by water, with a canal flowing through it and a major harbour and marina, Madinat Al Arab will feature resorts, retail, commercial spaces, public spaces, a broad mix of residences and an integrated transport system including light rail and a sophisticated road network. Located near the planned Jebel Ali Airport, and with direct access to Sheikh Zayed Road, Jebel Ali Free Zone and Abu Dhabi, the city will be fully accessible on a local and international scale.

The first phase of Madinat Al Arab (30%) was unveiled to a select invited group of private property and investment institutions from the UAE and GCC in July 2005. Within five days it was completely sold out for over Dh13 billion, demonstrating its appeal as one of the most exciting real estate developments in the world.

This Guide features a selection of Nakheel's major projects. More information about these or other Nakheel projects can be had at:

Nakheel Call Centre
P.O. Box 17777, Dubai
United Arab Emirates

Tel: +971 4 3903333
Fax: +971 4 3903314
Email: info@nakheel.ae
Website: www.nakheel.ae

74

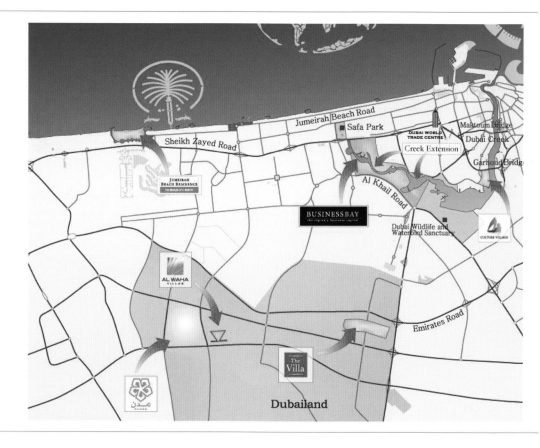

Founded in 2004, **Dubai Properties** is a member of Dubai Holding and operates with the express aim of conceiving unique communities that add value for the customer and contribute towards the growth of Dubai. The portfolio of projects handled by Dubai Properties is diverse and represents the highest quality of real estate in the region.

In 2006 Dubai Properties was granted Freehold Status under the articles of the Dubai Property Law, Article (4) specifically stated that non-GCC citizens are able to purchase freehold property in areas especially designated by H.H. Sheikh Mohammed bin Rashid Al Maktoum, UAE Vice President and Prime Minister and the Ruler of Dubai. In 2007 the employee strength of Dubai Properties was 1100 and the company continues to expand.

Dubai Properties projects include:

- **Jumeirah Beach Residence** - a sprawling 1.7 km waterfront, considered the largest single phase residential development in the world.
- **Business Bay** which covers an area of 64 million sq ft along the extension of the creek and will offer world-class infrastructure.
- **The Villa** at Dubailand - a residential retreat spread over 35 million sq ft and offers Spanish-style villas hacienda-style residential communities.
- **Culture Village** which covers an area of 40 million sq ft will include a residential, commercial and retail district in an intellectually stimulating environment.
- **Tijara Town** which covers 20 million sq ft and offers integrated office, showroom, warehouse, and apartments as one unit to improve operational efficiency.
- **Mudon** which incorporates five individual cities - Baghdad, Beirut, Damascus, Cairo, and Marrakech - within one large city, covering an area of 73 million sq ft.

In addition to the freehold master developments, Dubai Properties portfolio comprises a variety of leasing projects like diverse residential complexes, low-end housing communities and retail developments like The Walk at JBR and Bay Avenue at Business Bay. Its also includes joint ventures and partnerships within the educational, facilities management and real estate sector.

Jumeirah Beach Residence

Jumeirah Beach Residence, Dubai

The sprawling waterfront community of Jumeirah Beach Residence is the largest single phase residential development in the world. It features 36 residential towers, four hotel towers and four beach clubs.

The development offers a wide selection of residential units ranging from studio, one, two, three, and four bedroom apartments with sea view, marina view, and other views to suit different budgets and needs. Jumeirah Beach Residence will be one of the most extraordinary residential and holiday destinations in the Middle East.

It is a uniquely-themed environment combining the styles of Mediterranean and local architecture, complimented by landscaped plazas and children's play areas, fountains and courtyards.

Key Dates: Completion and handover, 2007

Location: Jumeirah Beach Road

Project Size: 5 million sq ft

Project Value: AED 7.3 billion / USD 2 billion

Type of Units: Penthouse, duplex, loft, studio, 1, 2, 3, 4 bedroom apartments

Key Features: 770,000 sq ft of retail space, over 400 outlets including 45 restaurants, 36 residential towers and 4 hotels, health clubs and swimming pools, kindergartens, medical centres and play areas.

The Walk

The Walk features an outdoor shopping concept in a uniquely-themed environment complimented by landscaped plazas and children's play areas, fountains and courtyards. Divided into two main levels comprising Grade Level and Plaza Level, The Walk encompasses over 350 retail units. The Walk is easily accessible from car parks, residential buildings and the hotels. Retail outlets are located along the Beach Drive, Marina Drive, and in the plazas around the residential towers.

Unit Type / Sizes		
Studio	505 units	(Area range: 600-640 sq ft)
One Bedroom	1276 units	(Area range: 924-1317 sq ft)
Two Bedrooms	2511units	(Area range: 1214-1400 sq ft)
Three Bedrooms	1868 units	(Area range: 1770-2335 sq ft)
Four Bedrooms	400 units	(Area range: 2641-3031 sq ft)
Duplex	76 units	(Area range: 2,982-5,511 sq ft)
Terrace Apartments	68 units	(Area range: 2,700-4,500 sq ft)
Lofts	140 units	(Area range: 1959-2443 sq ft)
Penthouses	72 units	(Area range: 5527-6261 sq ft)

Business Bay

Business Bay

Developed along the lines of Manhattan of New York or the Ginza of Tokyo, Business Bay will provide the best possible commercial environment to regional and international companies, investors and multinational businesses.

Business Bay will offer world-class infrastructure, design, urban planning, architecture and perfect environmental balance. It is one of the few developments that offer freehold office towers at the emerging centre of Dubai's new business district along the new Creek.

The lifestyle of Business Bay is positioned as urban, self-sustaining and business-oriented, catering to the corporate entities setting up base here. It also offers a sophisticated and fulfilling community lifestyle to residents.

Key Dates	Expected completion of Creek Extension: mid-2007
	Expected completion of Phase I: 2015
Location	Creek side – Located between Sheikh Zayed Road and Al Khail Road, between interchanges 1 and 2
Project Size	64 million sq ft
Project Value	AED 110 billion / USD 30 billion
Type of Units	Residential units (21.7%), commercial (15.3%) and mixed-use units (63%)
Key Features	A city built around the newly extended Creek
	Accessible from all major Dubai highways
	Expected population of 191,000, around 240 world-class towers to be completed in 2015
	Public areas and amenities such as parks, schools, security, medical facilities
	Retail, recreational and entertainment features
	Residential and Commercial units

- **The Executive Towers** comprise 11 towers: nine residential towers, one commercial tower known as Aspect Tower; and one hotel called the Business Bay Hotel. The apartments come equipped with modern amenities, high-tech facilities and internationally designed interior spaces that embody superb architectural innovation and breathtaking views of the winding Creek.
- **Business Bay Hotel** is an upscale 303-room luxury hotel situated in the heart of Business Bay developed by Dubai Properties and managed by an international luxury hotel chain providing guests with superior services and facilities. The hotel will feature trendy coffee shops, two specialty restaurants and tea lounge.
- **Bay Avenue** is a Creek side arena offering two levels of outdoor retail space, featuring waterfront cafes and restaurants, in addition to prestigious boutiques and showrooms. Complete with world-class infrastructure consisting of landscaped plazas, restaurants and cafes, children's play areas, sporting facilities and essential services, it creates a place for everyone to work, relax, shop, and dine.

Culture Village

The Villa, Dubailand

Culture Village

Culture Village is a mixed-use master development with wide open spaces, traditional wind towers, cobblestone walkways, unique sculptures, waterways topped with bridges. It will feature creek-side restaurants and cafés, a maritime museum, and a dockyard where traditional dhow building will be on display.

The residential district will feature traditional low- to medium-rise buildings and the commercial district will house cultural institutions, schools, academies for art, music, dance, pottery and other crafts. A rustic traditional souk, offering Arabian crafts, antiques, and spices and herbs, will be the focal point of the retail district.

Key Dates	Expected completion of Phase I: 2008
Location	Along the Dubai Creek next to the Garhoud Bridge
Project Size	40 million sq ft
Project Value	AED 50 billion/USD 13 billion
Type of Units	Studio, 1, 2, 3 and 4 bedroom apartments
Key Features	Exhibition hall, international academies of art and music, art galleries, maritime museum, libraries, traditional souk, residential, commercial, retail units

The Villa, Dubailand

The Villa is an enchanting residential retreat, inspired by generous spaces for outdoor living, the coolness and tranquility of Spanish-style courtyard housing and an environment alive with the sound of water from fountains in squares and from waterfalls cascading over rocky outcrops.

This residential community offers Spanish-style villas surrounded by a mystical desert landscape, ideal for those looking for tranquility from the main city area or the main highway. The residences at The Villa feature 4, 5 and 6 bedroom Spanish-style courtyard villas with terraces that offer views of the surrounding lush landscape and waterways.

With walkways and horse trails incorporated into the landscape, winding their way around the attractive desert landscape, restaurants, shops and pools all within walking distance of the villas, it combines a relaxed and serene lifestyle with the Spanish countryside experience.

Key dates	Expected completion date: 2008
Location	Dubailand
Project Size	35 million sq ft
Project Value	AED 6 billion / USD 1.7 billion
Type of Units	4, 5 and 6 bedroom
Key Features	Tranquil Spanish-style
	Infinite water features and private courtyards

Bay Square

Supreme community living facilities

Fine dining restaurants and cafes

- **The Haciendas** comprises of exclusive villas with manicured exterior spaces creating an attractive garden environment in a landscape of meandering water channels.
- **The Ponderosa** offers ranch style living with private courtyards, stable buildings, central pools and fountains punctured by rocky outcrops and waterfalls.
- **The Aldea** is an intimately planned town and courtyard housing with beautifully patterned streets, pathways, pools and fountains.
- **The Centro** is the focus of the community where shaded arcades fringe the cobbled square with its celebratory fountains in a vibrant mix of clubhouse, cafes, restaurants, shops and community facilities.

Bay Square

Bay Square is a trendy, mixed-use community within Business Bay. The entire development will be a pedestrian-only zone, and will include walkways over canals, a central plaza with unique water attractions, and a state-of-the-art gym.

Bay Square will cater to modern residents and retailers, a distinctive component of Bay Square will be its unique appeal to commercial investors seeking a creative and less corporate lifestyle and work ambience.

Bay Square's cafes, restaurants, and shops will overflow onto the pavements all along the waterline, creating a vivacious atmosphere day and night as tenants and visitors enjoy the open air atmosphere.

Key Dates	Completion and handover in 2009
Location	Business Bay
Project Size	5 million sq ft
Project Value	AED 4 billion / USD 1 billion
Type of Units	studios, 1 bedroom apartments, and loft-style apartments
Key Features	1 Boutique hotel
	1 Residential building
	11 mixed use buildings
	Rooftop and terrace apartments
	Commercial office space
	Retail space
	Pedestrian-only zone
	Walkways over canals
	Central plaza with unique water attractions
	Cafes, restaurants, and shops

Al Waha Villas

Al Waha Villas

Al Waha Villas is an exclusive gated residential community at the heart of Dubailand. A luxurious enclave of 260 Mediterranean-styled exclusive villas set among endless rows of towering palm trees and manicured gardens.

With its unique lines and curves, terracotta roofs, warm colors and cobbled driveways, Al Waha Villas is a stunning architectural concept in a backdrop of perennial blue skies.

The residences feature 2, 3 and 4 bedroom villas with terraces that offer views of the surrounding lush landscape and waterways.

Key Dates	Completion and handover, May 30th 2008
Location	Dubailand
Project Size	1,467,724.25 sq ft
Project Value	AED 735 million / USD 204.2 million
Type of Units	4, 3 & 2 bedroom villas
Key Features	Clubhouse, community swimming pool, Spanish style, gated community walkways

Dubai Properties
Office No:155, Building 7
Dubai Internet City
United Arab Emirates

Tel: +971 4 3911114
Fax: +971 4 3904640
Website: www.dubai-properties.ae

Index at the Dubai International Financial Centre

Union Properties PJSC (UP), one of the United Arab Emirates' leading property investment developers, started as Union Property Private Limited in 1987 and floated as a public limited company in 1993. UP delivers superior and comprehensive range of developments with a project portfolio of some of the most unique landmark commercial, residential and leisure developments in the country, acknowledged internationally.

Celebrating 20 Years of growth, innovation, motivation and attention to detail

UP started out with a vision strongly focused on creating a portfolio of excellence, the goal was to make a difference with a unique approach, by going beyond the norm. And that is what was achieved over the last two decades. Today, UP are recognised as trusted developers, responsible for some of Dubai's finest properties and creators of some of the best investment opportunities.

In 1987, UP net assets were worth AED one million and in 2006 the company represented an annual turnover of more than AED 2.5 billion, with net assets of more than AED 4.5 billion and projects under construction worth AED 13 billion and still growing rapidly.

As part of the Emirates Bank Group, UP has the solid support of a leading financial institution, an outstanding reputation for professionalism and integrity throughout the United Arab Emirates serving public institutions, multinational corporations, the business community and the private sector.

UP's success is based on six basic principles that form the foundation of its ethical code. Quality, service, innovation, care, trust and diversity are embedded in every venture it undertakes.

With over 24 projects, the company has created a portfolio of iconic landmarks in commercial, residential and leisure developments, from high-rise towers to multi-use complexes, hotels and theme parks. Index, Limestone House, MotorCity, Green Community, UPTOWN Mirdiff, Net.community and The Tower are but some of the renowned UP developments.

Index

Index is an 80 storey multi-purpose tower with state-of-the-art offices designed for multinational corporations and luxury apartments for those who expect exceptional living. The construction of Index started in 2006 and is planned to be completed in 2009. Index is the first of a new era of 'intelligent buildings' that are destined to be the skyscrapers of the future.

Limestone House

Index elegantly combines 25 floors of office space, 40 floors for apartments, in addition to 7 dedicated for penthouses and 3 levels for exclusive retails outlets. 'Minimalism can refer to the extreme simplicity of a work of art. The Index building is simplicity personified.' Index is a landmark building in a prime location within the rapidly developing Dubai International Financial Centre (DIFC).

- Index is the creation of reputed award-winning architects Foster & Partners, a leading firm of architects in the United Kingdom.

- The concept of a multi-functional tower ensures that the building is utilized 24/7; that it is never vacant, increasing security and energy efficiency; holistically a building that exudes good vibes and energy.

- The tower is oriented east to west to maximize views north over the Financial Centre and south to the desert. This orientation reduces solar gain, with the building core mass absorbing heat to reduce mechanical ventilation loads.

Limestone House

Limestone House is the creation of a vision to construct prominence and to design an incomparable standard of living focusing on opulence, style and traditional luxury. The vision of the project is to provide exclusive luxury apartments for a select few discerning buyers. Featuring an exceptional blend of architectural décor influenced by ancient Arabia and the exotic Mediterranean, this unique residence has been designed to the time-honoured specifications of the master stonemason, with window length, breadth and height determined by the traditional dimensions of masonry blocks.

- Limestone House is located in a commanding position within Dubai International Financial Centre (DIFC).

- The development is a glorious representation of highly distinguished, luxurious living for the elite few, through the inclusion of exquisite marble and timber finishes.

- Great care has been taken to ensure the space within each home exudes classic style and functionality.

- Exquisite craftsmanship can be seen from the timber flooring to the mosaic tiles in the bathroom and the fully fitted, elegant yet practical kitchen designed with an exacting eye for detail.

MotorCity

- The amenities feature complete concierge facilities to health and wellness offerings, including an indoor lap pool, state-of-the-art fitness centre, Jacuzzi plus separate male and female changing facilities with steam rooms in each.

- A tranquil, private terrace with a sunken garden provides a natural environment in which to relax.

- To ensure the utmost privacy and personalized entry for the apartments residence there will be exclusive lift access serving a limited number of apartments with secured parking entry and access control to operate the designated elevator to the resident's home.

MotorCity

MotorCity, is a development based on a unique automobile and motor sport theme that includes residential, business, sports and leisure opportunities. MotorCity is in fact 'a city within a city' with five project components over a land of approximately 38,000,000 sq ft, located on Emirates Road.

- **Green Community MotorCity**
  Family home development that includes family villas, townhouses, and bungalows. In addition, the development will feature luxurious terraced apartments overlooking an artificial lake. The development will be gated and offer retail opportunities and recreation centres. Construction is due for completion and handover in 2009.

- **UPTOWN MotorCity**
  An apartment development that will provide recreational areas and other community amenities such as parks and schools. The residential units will include a mix of studio, one, two and three bedroom apartments with exclusive 4 bedroom townhouses in the crescent area. Construction is due for completion and handover in 2009.

- **Dubai Autodrome**
  Already operational, the facility features a 5.39 km FIA certified track with supporting services (pit garages, grandstand, race administration, medical centres, etc.). The Dubai Autodrome also includes a kartdrome and a race school. A host of businesses use the track year round for events such as product launches, corporate events and concerts, to name a few.

- **Business Park MotorCity**
  Offers numerous investment and development opportunities for companies directly and indirectly related to the automotive and motor sport industries. This component of MotorCity will also feature the Automall complex that will include three major buildings connected to each other; a 3 storey showroom, a 38 storey office building and a hotel. The Business Park MotorCity is divided into 3 main districts: the Retail Commercial District, the Auto Commercial District and the Applied Technologies District.

Green Community - Villas

Green Community - Hotel and Retail

- **F1 Theme Park**

  The F1 Theme Park will be an edutainment destination for the whole family. The USD 460 million development spreads 300,000 sq m, leaving everyone feeling the exhilarating and exciting thrill of the F1 brand experience.

Green Community

Green Community is a quality development by Properties Investment LLC, a joint venture company between Union Properties PJSC and Dubai Investments PJSC. The development provides a way of life within a working and living secure community which encompasses landscaped gardens, stone streets and a relatively traffic free environment. Covering 67 lush hectares of residential, leisure, retail, and commercial properties the development prides itself on its modern and beautiful surroundings with natural greenery being the key to peace and tranquility.

With Townhouse units, Family Villas, Luxury Villas, Garden Apartments, Terrace Apartments and Lake Apartments, Green Community includes various services for its residents:

- The Market: community shopping centre
- Courtyard by Marriott Dubai Green Community
- Marriott Executive Apartments Dubai Green Community
- The Children's Garden: kindergarten and nursery

Green Community West

Following the success of Green Community, perhaps the most well received development of its kind in the region, Green Community West has been launched. Built around the same philosophy and attention to detail that made Green Community such a unique residential development, Green Community West will feature an exceptional choice of residences, each one distinctly different from each other.

Nestled in a tranquil, traffic-free environment with cobbled road, pleasing walkways, manicured gardens and acres of open space, Green Community West is sprinkled with recreation centres and every other element required for idyllic community living. It's located just 40km from the heart of Dubai but a world away from big city life, and is again a development where living comes naturally.

- Located next to Green Community in the Dubai Investments Park on Emirates Road.
- Spread across a 100-hectare plot size, Green Community West has 836 units featuring Bungalows, Family Villas, Luxury Villas and Garden Apartments

Community living at UPTOWN Mirdiff

Architecturally designed along the lines of an ancient spa town, UPTOWN Mirdiff, built in the heart of one of Dubai's most tranquil locations, promises an excellent variety of residential properties, play areas and recreation facilities nestled within landscaped gardens and public parks. Superbly appointed Townhouses, stylish Rowhouses and five distinct apartment styles are planned around a Grand Piazza, the centerpiece of the community.

Abundant with neighbourly appeal and filled with convenient shopping and dining outlets, UPTOWN Mirdiff is a delightful, secure, family living environment complete with:

- Three Bedroom Townhouses
- Three Bedroom Rowhouses
- Studio Apartments
- One Bedroom Apartments
- Two Bedroom Apartments
- A Shopping Centre
- Park and Landscape area
- Mosque
- Primary School

Union Properties

P.O.Box 24649, Dubai, United Arab Emirates

Green Community, Dubai Investment Park

Tel: +971 4 8851555

Fax: + 971 4 8852666

Email: contactus@up.ae

Website: www.up.ae

www.tameer.net

Tameer Holding was established in 1991 engaging in miscellaneous business activities. In 2002 the establishment decided to concentrate solely on the real estate sector shortly before forming a strategic partnership with Al-Rajhi Investment Group. Today, the firm's investment portfolio in the market totals over AED 150 billion.

Tameer Holding had entered the thriving UAE property market in Dubai with the "Princess Tower", one of the world's tallest residential towers, located in Dubai Marina. Other projects located in Dubai include the "Dana 1 & Dana 2" projects , "Al Jawzaa" in International City, "The Regal Tower", the "Silver Tower" and the "Platinum Towers" in Business Bay, "The Palace Towers" in Dubai Silicon Oasis, "Al Shahd" in the Emirates Hills, the "Elite Residence" in Dubai Marina and "The Imperial Residence" in Jumeirah Village.

Tameer has entered other cities in the UAE with mega projects and developments like Al Salam City and the Emirates Modern Industrial Area (EMIA) in Umm Al Quwain city. Al Ameera Village in Ajman city and the "Tameer Towers" and the "Gate" projects in Shams Abu Dhabi located on Reem Island. In addition to these projects in the UAE, Tameer has other international developments including the ground breaking USD 250 million Jordanian project called "Al Majd City" and Tameer's largest project to date, "Al Hanaa City" based in Libya's Eastern Valley, covering over 40 sq km, which includes residential and commercial towers, business centres, and tourism facilities.

In a short space of time, this firm has managed to launch and complete some of the region's most advanced construction developments the Middle East has ever seen. Their objective of developing luxurious projects for all walks of life has enabled them to distinguish themselves from other firms and has ensured them the position of one of the UAE's leading property firms.

Al Salam City (Umm Al Quwain)

Al Salam City is a masterpiece of modern planning and a vision of the way all cities should be. The city has luxury villas, apartments, malls and shops, restaurants, mosques, schools, hotels, parks, office towers, cinemas, wide-ranging sports, a golf course, cultural and entertainment centers and parks, and a major, international downtown district that will be home to one of the largest malls in the UAE
- Situated between the Emirates Road and the Pan Emirates Highway in Umm Al Quwain
- Al Salam City covers a total area of 220 million square feet
- Just 15 minutes from Sharjah and 25 minutes from Dubai
- Wide selection of apartments, townhouses and luxury villas
- The commercial developments of the city was showcased during Cityscape 2007

Imperial Residence

Regal Tower

- The commercial strip of the city includes the Trade park zone, Iconic Mixed zone, Business Park zone and the Showrooms zone
- The Central Activity district which is going to be the main attraction of ASC with a total area of 3 million sq ft was also showcased during Cityscape
- The Central Activity district will comprise mainly of mixed use developments (Commercial & Residential components), commercial strip, commercial buildings, religious facilities, sports and recreation, educational institutes, cultural centers, public utility, roads and landscaping.
- Comprehensive facilities, including schools, hospitals, parks, gymnasiums, recreational and cultural centres
- Guest accommodation, indoor and outdoor swimming pools, sports courts, children's playgrounds and business centres
- Nursery monitoring via webcams and CCTV
- Internationally themed downtown district
- Golf courses
- Unique opportunity to create high returns on residential properties and retail space
- Freehold to GCC nationals and Leasehold available to all other nationalities as per UAQ Government Laws.

The Imperial Residence (Dubai)

This new residential tower, located at Jumeirah Village South overlooking the Al Khail Road and the Emirates Road, will feature 2000 spaciously constructed villas and townhouses and include an exceptional array of amenities and services.

The Imperial Residence's design reflects a past era where class and creativity in design was paramount, while still providing all the functional assets needed for modern living in a thriving metropolis.
- includes 569 residential units in a variety of studio, 1, 2 and 3 bedroom apartments
- includes a twin tower structure that will comprise of 28 floors that rise from a 4-storey podium
- spread over 1 million sq ft
- features a fashionable mixture of Victorian and Art Deco design, mimicking a classical era of architecture from America's early to mid twentieth century
- this new project will be situated between Sheikh Zayed Road and Emirates Road, and offer easy access to all of Dubai's central and iconic locations

Regal Tower (Dubai)

Regal Tower located at Business Bay is an ideal setting at the heart of Dubai's business community, with a variety of office spaces.
- 32 floors, 258 units, 1 recreation floor and 3 basement levels
- Retail and commercial outlets

Silver Tower

Princess Tower

- Lake view available
- Terrace area with lush landscaping
- Banquet hall for special events
- Fully equipped health club
- Mini golf putting area
- State-of-the-art business centre
- Freehold to all nationalities as per Dubai Holdings regulations

Silver Tower (Dubai)

The Silver Tower is a freehold office tower that stands tall at the waterfront exit of Business Bay with unrivaled views of the lake and city.

- Consists of 34 floors, 2 basements + G + 31 storeys office tower
- It is a total of 27 floors + 4 parking lots for 793 cars
- Total built up area: 726722 sq ft
- Height 147.5m (Top of feature)
- 6 high speed elevators
- Mini golf course on the fifth floor
- Covered swimming pool
- International standard multi gym
- Waterside restaurants and cafes
- Retail therapy provided

Platinum Towers - Business Bay Dubai

It consists of 2 adjacent towers and will be located in the heart of Business Bay. As the name already reflects, it will be very modern and will project a specific level of luxury.

- 1 residential tower – 24 floors
- 1 office tower – 26 floors
- Podium – 3 floors + 3 basement floors + 1 ground floor
- 984 car space available
- Gym+ health club+ shopping mall area + retail shops+ restaurants
- Interlinked with the office tower by a 3-storey podium and last 3 floors
- Five star hotel of over 180 rooms includes 52 serviced apartments

Elite Residence

Al Jawzaa

Princess Tower (Dubai)

Princess Tower is one of the world's tallest residential towers, a fitting companion for such wonders as the Burj Al Arab, Madinat Jumeirah and the Palm Jumeirah.

- In the heart of Dubai Marina City, close to the Emirates Golf Club, the American University, Dubai Media City, Dubai Internet City and the Palm Jumeirah
- 107 floors and 414 metres high, Princess Tower offers a choice of stunning 1,2,3 bedroom apartments, 4 bedroom penthouses, duplex apartments and a villa
- 10 elevators, maid's room, business centre, private car parking for each resident
- Freehold available to all nationalities as per Emaar regulations.

Elite Residence (Dubai)

One of the Middle East's most exclusive and desirable addresses, the Elite Residence provides stunning 1 and 2 bedroom apartments, 3 and 4 bedroom penthouses and a villa. It offers the last word in luxury, elegance and service to the discerning few.

- Situated at the heart of Dubai Marina, near the Palm Jumeirah and the Mall of the Emirates, and ideally placed close to the Emirates Golf Club, the American University, Dubai Media City, Dubai Internet City and Dubai International Airport
- 91 floors and 380 metres high, the Elite Residence is home to 695 apartments, penthouses and a villa, all designed and fitted to the very highest standards of design and construction
- Luxury reception, temperature controlled swimming pools, gymnasium and health spa
- Freehold available to all nationalities as per Emaar regulations.

Al Jawzaa (Dubai)

Al Jawzaa Tower lies at the bustling heart of Dubai's International City, a byword for cosmopolitan lifestyles, with its extraordinary replicas of world famous monuments and buildings.

- Located in the international city (phase 3)
- 180 studio units, 1 & 2 bedroom apartments
- 6 shops
- Swimming pools, gymnasium, health spa, luxury reception, etc
- Freehold to all nationalities, as per Nakheel rules and regulations.

Palace Towers

Palace Towers (Dubai)

Palace Towers offer superb residential accommodation and easy access to the business area of Dubai Silicon Oasis, the world's leading purpose-built high technology park for the micro electronics and semi conductor industries.

- Located at the heart of Dubai Silicon Oasis, on the Emirates Road, within easy reach of Dubailand, the Arabian Ranches and the Autodrome
- Offers 424 studio, 1 & 2 bedroom apartments
- 150 offices, 16 shops
- Restaurant, cafeteria, 2 swimming pools, 3 gymnasiums and banquet hall
- Freehold for UAE nationals/ GCC nationals, as per Dubai Silicon Oasis Regulations
- Leasehold for all other nationalities, as per Dubai Silicon Oasis Regulations.

Al Ameera Village (Ajman)

Its building techniques and modern facilities is an ideal choice for families of all nationalities.

- Conveniently located off the Emirates Road in Ajman
- 15 minutes from Dubai International Airport and Dubailand
- 41 traditionally designed residential buildings, hotel apartments, shopping malls, and commercial outlets
- Temperature controlled swimming pools, covered parking, health spa and prayer area
- Plots of land also available
- Freehold available to all nationalities as per Ajman Government Laws.

TAMEER
P.O. Box 23936
Sharjah
United Arab Emirates

Tel: +971 6 5995000
Fax:+971 6 5995199
Email: info@tameer.net
Website: www.tameer.net

AL FARA'A
P R O P E R T I E S
Building Since 1980

The Manhattan

Backed by the strong values which are in line with internationally accepted standards of professionalism, ethics and quality, **Al Fara'a Properties** is growing fast and is well on its way to becoming the UAE's most valued property development company.

The key strength that gives Al Fara'a Properties an edge over most of the other UAE based property development companies is the backing of Al Fara'a Construction Group, an integrated construction and property development solution provider with real state expertise spanning well over two decades. The group is committed in building excellence through quality partnerships with clients, consultants, government departments and the private sector to offer the best real estate value solutions under one roof.

Based in Dubai, Al Fara'a Properties comes as a flagship subsidiary of this group, successfully defining both residential and commercial space with an objective to maximize investor returns. With over 12,000 employees, vast experience and international presence, Al Fara'a understands the core insights of its customers coming from varied cultural and regional backgrounds. Al Fara'a is well on course of successfully satisfying these insights by building homes that combine luxury, quality and beauty. Whether someone is a first time buyer or a seasoned investor, Al Fara'a has established its strength to provide unsurpassed quality at the best value price.

Destined to become a landmark in the Jumeirah Village community, the design of the Manhattan draws its inspiration from the urbane residences of 1930's New York.

The Manhattan offers the discerning businessman the best possible address in Dubai. Jumeirah Village, situated between Emirates, Al Khail and Al Barsha Roads, is designed as a self-sustained community with its own business centres, characterized by distinctive modern towers offering a balance of retail, commercial and entertainment facilities.

Within walking distance are residential areas, recreational facilities, and every possible amenity to ensure a balanced lifestyle. Manhattan offers an easy lifestyle of unsurpassed quality in one geographic area, where one can live, work and play. Construction of the Manhattan has already started in October of 2007 along with the project launch.

Visa and Finance
The Manhattan is a 100% freehold property. All registered proprietors will be entitled to a UAE residence visa to be issued by the appropriate Dubai Government Authorities under their

Le Grand Chateau

standard Terms and Conditions. The Developer will assist registered owners to obtain mortgage funds from ADCB and Emirates Islamic Bank up to 90% as per the existing policy terms and conditions related to the project and subject to status.

Le Grand Château, the signature project, is set in the heart of the Jumeirah Village community, adjacent to a green belt, providing the ideal location within this sought after development.
Le Grand Château is inspired by the timeless appeal of the grand sixteenth century Châteaux of France's Loire Valley. A truly unique living environment, the townhouses, studios and apartments incorporate a distinctive design with modern innovation in units offering substantially more floor space than comparable developments.

The apartments overlook a beautifully landscaped inner courtyard, water features as well as a state-of the-art clubhouse. The luxurious majestic design of Le Grand Château is a fitting tribute to the quality and standard of craftsmanship you associate with the name Al Fara'a.

Al Fara'a launched and started construction of Le Grand Château in December 2006 and is well on the way to delivering the commitment. Jumeirah Village South is a master development of over 900 plots. Al Fara'a Properties is the first developer to start building in this amazing location.

Visa and Finance

Le Grand Chateau is a 100% freehold property. All registered proprietors will be entitled to a UAE residence visa to be issued by the appropriate Dubai Government Authorities under their standard Terms and Conditions. The Developer will assist registered owners to obtain mortgage funds from ADCB up to 90% as per the existing policy terms and conditions related to the project and subject to status.

Al Fara'a Properties
Suite 105, The Business Centre Building, Khalid Bin Waleed Street
Dubai
United Arab Emirates
Tel: +971 4 3961118
Fax: +971 4 3964448
Email: info@alfaraaproperties.com / contact@alfaraaproperties.com
Website: www.alfaraaproperties.com
Toll Free Number: 800-ALFARAA(2532722)

BUILT *on* TRUST

Goldcrest Dreams

ETA Star Property Developers LLC, a part of the ETA – ASCON conglomerate, is one of the leading property development companies in the Middle East. The company offers the whole gamut of services connected with property development, leasing and management of properties.

With the opening of the real estate market in the UAE to expatriate investors, ETA Star has embarked on a major programme to develop Commercial and Residential properties for the benefit of the local and expatriate population.

At present, the company is in the process of promoting freehold and leasehold properties at prime locations in Dubai including Dubai Marina, Jumeirah Lake Towers, DIFC, Palm Jumeirah, IMPZ, DIC and DMC. ETA Star's portfolio currently includes prestigious commercial and residential properties such as The Belvedere, The Palladium, Liberty House, Pearl Residence, Goldcrest Executive, Goldcrest Views-2, the 23 Marina and the recently announced Al Manara at Business Bay. ETA Star as a company believes in keeping the environment green; to the extent that their very first project had as much as 35% of the plot allocated for landscaping.

Goldcrest Dreams - Ajman

The four majestic residential towers of Goldcrest Dreams is being built in the newest mixed use development on the Emirates Highway, Ajman. Aptly named the Paradise Lakes, it caters to a wide range of tastes and preferences.

Located on the Emirates Highway, Goldcrest Dreams is:
- Twenty minutes drive from Dubai International Airport.
- Twenty minutes drive from Sharjah International Airport.
- Twenty five minutes drive from Dubai City Centre.

There will be ready access to shopping areas within Paradise Lakes.

The lobby of each block will be designed to impress
- Dreams 1 Bedroom
  Four different variations on the one bedroom apartments will ensure better choice.
- Dreams 2 Bedroom
  Large two bedroom apartment that are ideal for families.

The Summit

Facilities

- G + 4 Parking – 25 Floors
- Choice of single and double bedroom units
- Actual 100% ownership
- UAE residence visa
- Lakes, waterways and fountains
- Landscaped gardens
- Swimming pools
- Playground areas
- Security systems
- Satellite TV
- Neighbouring shopping mall

The Summit

Conceived as a trapezoidal form, The Summit lends itself to interestingly transforming perspectives from various vantage points, as it escalates. The higher end of the trapezoid splits itself to reveal a soaring spire that pierces the sky, beckoning a focal point for the district. Two majestic facades wrap around delicately, creating an architectural dialogue and composing a distinct visual treat.

An elegant, contemporary podium heralds the entrance. The entrance canopy is enhanced with an inviting water feature. The tower elevates itself to 38 stories with its peak soaring skywards. Capped by a crystalline glass enclosure, it distinguishes itself from the rest with a shimmering red glow that emulates an ever-burning torch of fire.

The state-of-the-art freehold offices at The Summit are built to meet the evolving business needs of future Dubai. The flexible open plan units can be custom-sized to the exact business needs of individual clients, starting from as less as 1000 sq. ft. Every office unit is well lit, well ventilated and offers picturesque views of the surrounding greenery and high-rise developments. The offices can avail high-speed broadband Internet connection and high security access systems. There is also the convenient option of private pantry and/or restroom. Every unit enjoys access to the leisure decks at podium level. Meticulous maintenance and complete business support is also offered.

Introducing Condo Offices
ETA Star has joined hands with Colliers International, a renowned international property management company to present a novel investment opportunity in the UAE and the Condo Offices - exclusively for The Summit investors.

Starhill Towers & Gallery

A special rental pool ensures guaranteed occupancy and takes care of everything, right from sourcing tenants, handling necessary paperwork and other legal matters so the investors are absolutely free from all leasing worries.

The Condo-Offices ensure attractive returns on fully built office spaces, starting from as less as 1000 sq. ft. Hence, the Condo-Offices at The Summit not only offer the opportunity to own a prime office property but also the rewarding prospect of building equity in the property.

The Summit offers world-class recreational and business amenities, making it a self-sustained business community. The podium flaunts a business centre with state-of-the-art information technology and dedicated round-the-clock services. A modern health club with gym, a clubhouse and a swimming pool deck make up the recreation zone. Located strategically at the roof level of the podium and the foot of the office tower, the recreation zone offers a picturesque view of the verdant Emirates Golf Club and the scenic Jumeirah beach.

At the podium level, shops extend from the spacious retail gallery to an outdoor landscaped area, facing Sheikh Zayed Road. This elegant facade also provides a spacious outdoor dining area for the cafes and restaurants at The Summit.

Starhill Towers & Gallery

Starhill Towers & Gallery is a unique business edifice that offers more than just freehold offices. It is a unique confluence of sense and sensibility. A mixed-use project comprising spectacular twin-towers, its outstanding business amenities are embellished with myriad leisure offerings. The luxurious 'Starhill Gallery' will offer a bouquet of exclusive experiences, from fashion, lifestyle, beauty and art to fine dining. A five-star hotel, hotel apartments and an array of recreational facilities go on to complete the "Bizort' experience.

Designed by the eminent DP Architects, Singapore, the twin towers are shaped to a convex curve with their elevations forming a wave-like appearance at the peak. The two tower blocks are connected by means of an open-to-sky garden belt that offers a spectacular view of the waterfront.

Starhill Towers & Gallery is strategically located in Business Bay, an ambitious master development envisioned by the ruler of Dubai, Sheikh Mohammed bin Rashid Al Maktoum. The 'city within the city' is deemed to turn Dubai into a leading global commercial and business centre.

Covering an area of 64 million sq ft, the Business Bay will host everything from commercial towers to luxurious recreation to mixed-use projects. All this amidst a spectacular landscape, bordering the Dubai Creek - the city's business lifeline.

Feast Zone

Adorn Zone

Pamper Zone

Muse Zone

The project will offer a highly business conducive atmosphere complete with world-class infrastructure for business from around the world who wish to establish a strong local presence in the region.

Zones at Starhill Gallery

The 'Feast' zone will offer an exotic array of culinary delights with international themed restaurants. A dramatic, stylish dining haven with a village charm, 'Feast' zone shall have uniquely designed restaurants, serving a mix of world-class cuisine and providing a display of culinary skills. All in an iconic atmosphere of new chic and contemporary lifestyle.

The 'Adorn' zone is an oasis of myriad fashion, lifestyle and home furnishing brands that are exciting and energetic. High street fashion brands from around the world will find their place at the 'Adorn' zone. Exclusive creations from some of UAE's finest and most innovative designers will also be featured.

The 'Pamper' zone is a wellness and beauty haven, which shall offer a variety of treatments including beauty therapies, nail bars and reflexology. There will be a wealth of services to pamper the senses while renowned beauty brands cater to every eclectic desire. 'Pamper', a zone deveted entirely to beauty and health, is designed not only to rejuvenate the body but also refresh the soul.

The 'Muse' zone celebrates the splendour of fine art, photography, sculptures and antiques. The 'Photographer's Gallery' shall display an international collection of contemporary photography. The 'Loft Gallery" shall house art and sculptures by renowned national and international artists.

ETA Star Property Developers LLC
4B Hamarian Centre
P.O.Box 29193, Dubai
United Arab Emirates

Tel: +971 4 2687222
Toll Free: 800-ETA STAR (800 382 7827)
Fax: +971 4 2623291
Website: www.etastar.com

KM PROPERTIES®

Member of KM Holding

PARK LANE Hotel and Commercial Tower

B2B Tower

KM Properties, the real estate arm of KM Holding, is strengthening its position as a market leading developer by focusing on the core business of property development locally and internationally to achieve high returns. In July 2007, just a week after the announcement of Law 8 on Property and Escrow account ruling by Dubai Land Department, KM Properties became the first Developer in Dubai, approved and licensed as Real Estate Developer, to promote and sell development properties by the Dubai Economic Department.

KM Properties offers Escrow facilities on its multiple properties. The escrow partner is National Bank of Dubai.

"KM Properties has worked closely with RERA (Real Estate Regulatory Authority) since its formation in the summer and was one of the first developers to offer Escrow financing, thus offering complete peace of mind to would-be investors. This has had a strong impact on its reputation in the market, and is a role model for other private developers to follow in their foot step" added Marwan Bin Ghalita, Executive Director of the Real Estate Regulatory Authority.

The foremost objective of KM Properties towards investors is to provide them the opportunity to use a unique, safe investment business model developed by the company where real estate property becomes a low risk investment, but, with massive potential for return profits and growing yields so investors continue to enjoy healthy returns on their investments. In their recent Cityscape Dubai 2007 presence, investors made off with 111% capital gains within 72 hours when KM Properties pre-launched its newest top-selling property development the TAMANI Arts Offices.

The company owns a large number of properties in the UAE of exceptional quality and value with a selection of properties that can only be described as deluxe due to the high quality of accommodation, decoration and equipment provided, as well as locations and views.

In the UAE, its property portfolio includes iconic projects at the Business Bay development: the 33-storey **Park Lane Hotel and Commercial Tower**, the **ARTISAN CLUSTER** comprising the **Tamani Arts Hotel** and **TAMANI Arts Offices**; and the **B2B Tower**. Another mixed-use commercial and residential development is the **El Matador Tower** that will rise in the Jumeirah Village community.

TAMANI Arts Offices at the Artisan Cluster
A prime property for long term investment, the TAMANI Arts Offices is an influential and sophisticated business tower.

El Matador Tower

TAMANI Art Offices, Artisan Cluster

The Artisan Cluster, spanning a built-up area of approximately two million square feet, is an exceptional development near Burj Dubai consisting of clusters of iconic towering structures that comprise hotels, commercials towers and residential buildings. The structural wonder is designed by Terry Farrell and Partners; whom KM Properties signed a strategic joint venture in July 2007. They are the renowned designers of Greenwich Millennium Dome in London. The Artisan Cluster tower designs are truly reflective of an artisan's love for unique beauty enveloped in varied motifs and themes.

Tamani Arts Offices at the Artisan Cluster is a lakeside property situated next to residential properties and ensuring higher returns. It offers an unobstructed view of Burj Dubai, the world's tallest structure, while being surrounded by lake waters making the property value more appreciable. Serviced and managed by Tamani Hotels and Resorts, this 100% ultra modern infrastructure assures of a definite increase in property value appreciation.

International plans

KM Holding, through its real estate development company KM Properties currently has a portfolio of projects in Dubai. While these projects are under construction, the company has already begun looking at the international market, starting with the Middle East region, particularly the Kingdom of Saudi Arabia. A five star commercial mixed-use tower is planned in the Jeddah Waterfront area.

In addition, the company is also considering projects in Asia, particularly India. Additionally, its sister company, the TAMANI Hotels and Resorts, is planning to roll out 12 to 15 four and five star hotels in the next five years in locations such as India, Qatar, Bahrain, Saudi Arabia and Malaysia. The first hotel to fly the TAMANI flag is TAMANI Hotel Marina which is slated for opening in late 2007.

KM Properties
P.O. Box: 42035, Dubai,
United Arab Emirates

Toll Free : 800-KMP (567) (for UAE only)
For International Users : +971 4 2951615
Fax : +971 4 2951484
Website: www.km-properties.com

A·C·I

Alternative Capital Invest

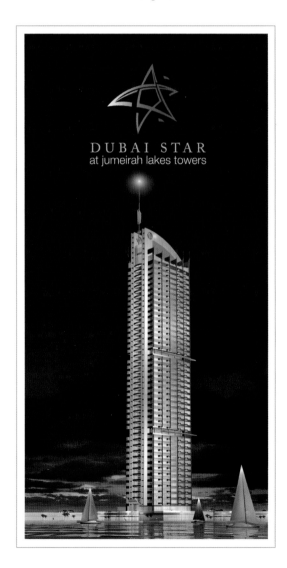

Alternative Capital Invest (ACI) Group is one of Germany's leading providers of alternative investment solutions. Established in Dubai in 2004, the company soon realized the potential of the local real estate market. The father and son team of Uwe Lohmann and Robin Lohmann have injected an impressive investment in areas such as Jumeirah Lakes Towers, Business Bay and City of Arabia to name a few.

ACI Real Estate has achieved a lot since its establishment. They have about 4,000 customers and most of them are German speaking Europeans. ACI maintains very high standards and it meets the demand of the investors. Therefore, ACI ensures that the basic amenities provided to the end users are up to the mark and meet global standards.

To remain competitive in this market, ACI aims to develop projects in prime locations in and around Dubai to attract investors from all parts of the world.

Dubai Star

Located at the Jumeirah Lakes Towers, Dubai Star is one of the outstanding structures that will dominate the immediate landscape.

Surrounded by the spectacular view of the deep blue yonder and eternal sunshine, Dubai Star is a heavenly place to unwind. The tower is designed to reflect the architectural theme of the future through a fusion of elements, while retaining a unique style and aesthetic expression of its own.

Facilities
- Retail Space – a place where professionals can enjoy their own space, in every sense of the word.
- Office Spaces – Well planned offices. Cabling to facilitate high-speed internet access with future technology-ready features.
- Residential Luxury – Contemporary furnishings, latest amenities and a cosmopolitan look are the key highlights of this tower.
- Grand Lobby Area – The tower welcomes its guests and clients from its grand lobby. Stylish finish and a peaceful environment is what Dubai Star is all about.
- Recreational Facilities – Whether you are looking to rejuvenate yourself in the spa or treat yourself to the Arabian delicacies or simply take a dip in the pool, the tower offers a level of attentive personal service and design freedom found only in the finest residences in the world.
- Utilities & Services – The tower offers the finest international facilities and services. Cutting

edge technology, business services and amenities are available 24/7.

- Scenic view – Offering breathtaking views of an expansive horizon that changes a million hues as the day goes by, the apartments are thoughtfully laid out to create a sense of space and comfort.
- Central air conditioning
- Ceramic floor tiles
- Solid core entry door with security view hole
- Walk-in closets
- Insulated and double glazed windows
- Tiled balconies
- Overhead lighting

'Q' Sami Tower

'Q' Sami Tower provides the best working environment where modernity meets elegance. To keep one's business moving with the time, the tower features state-o-the-art VOIP technology, wireless Internet technology as well as intelligent, fully intergrated management systems.

Conducting business in Business Bay starts at the luxurious 'Q' Sami Tower, designed to the highest standards and offering a business lifestyle unimaginable. From the superb architectural style of each office space to the breathtaking views just outside, life at the 'Q' Sami Tower is intended for people who seek luxury in a vibrant community of like-minded individuals.

The 'Q' Sami Tower offers a successful lifestyle equipped with every amenity needed to make business a real pleasure. Top range recreational facilities at the 'Q' Sami Tower, including state-of-the-art leisure facilities and retail shops, provide the end-user with a positive and healthy work environment.

Victory Bay

Business Bay offers a successful lifestyle equipped with every amenity needed to make living and working a real pleasure. Apart from ensuring effective infrastructural development, Business Bay is the cornerstone of the new economic push to extend the international role of the UAE. Living at Business Bay means being part of the future.

Victory Bay is a state-of-the-art, 20-storey, x-shaped freehold office tower. Offering 75,702 sq m of floor space, the Tower's blue structural glazing that encases the floor to ceiling glass façade ensures the building offers an abundance of natural light across all office spaces.

Victory Bay provides office spaces that can be easily divided into smaller modules without losing

Victory Bay

easy accessibility. The tower features state-of-the-art technology, including CCTV with 24-hour monitoring, Wi-Fi, high-speed Internet connection, 24-hour security and 24-hour maintenance.

The tower offers a gamut of recreational facilities featuring a restaurant and café with outdoor seating on the podium level, a fully equipped gymnasium, sauna, rest area, change and locker facilities and outdoor swimming pool. The tower also offers fine dining restaurants, cafes and shopping outlets for some retail therapy.

Victory Bay Tower lies at the heart of the Business Bay area that overlooks two main streets and is in close proximity to the Burj Dubai Area, the Dubai International Financial Centre, Dubai International Airport and Jebel Ali Free Zone.

Overlooking Sheikh Zayed Road, the Victory Bay Tower is adjacent to the main entrance of Business Bay providing access to Dubai's main artery with access to all major road links. An additional benefit will be the nearby metro station.

Alternative Capital Invest
LEADING GERMAN DEVELOPER IN THE U.A.E.

Alternative Capital Invest
Umm Suqueim, Jumeirah 3
P.O Box 212049, Dubai
United Arab Emirates

Tel: +971 4 4079400,
Fax: +971 4 3954424
Email: info@aci-dubai.net
Website: www.aci-dubai.net

Real Estate
LEADING GERMAN DEVELOPER IN THE U.A.E.

La Hoya Bay Master plan - PHASE I

Khoie Properties formed in 2003 comprises a group of companies that own, develop and sell real estate projects.

It also sets itself apart by adopting a unique marketing strategy focusing on competitive sale prices that are within the reach of many for ownership or investment. In all its dealings, Khoie strives to achieve the highest degree of professional integrity and transparency.

The company has established a niche position in the waterfront development sector with a major programme of mixed use residential, commercial and leisure projects on the newly created Marjan Island in Ras Al Khaimah, UAE.

Construction is currently underway on two projects – La Hoya Bay Residence and La Hoya Bay Business Village, with further projects for a marina, luxury hotels and apartments currently in the design stage.

In addition, the company provides various support services and products in synergy with its core project development activity.

Current Projects

La Hoya Bay
La Hoya Bay is on the prime location of Marjan Island, Ras Al Khaimah. The total development area is 2 million square feet with an approximate project size of AED 2.9 billion. To be released in phases, the complete development will be set within gated communities with fully landscaped gardens and large beachfronts. The communities will include high-tech security, pools and health club facilities, ample parking, retails outlets and numerous other facilities. Units will be finished to a high international specification. Details of current projects are found below. Future phases will include a hotel and marina development and luxury one-unit-per floor 'penthouses'.

La Hoya Bay Residence
1310 spacious studio, one, two and three bedroom apartments, housed within seven G+7 blocks, set on a prime waterfront site of 629 thousand square foot. The development will be enhanced with fashionable retail outlets and health clubs, and includes a floating restaurant accessible via a floating promenade. Total unit prices range from between approximately AED 0.4mn to AED 2.1mn.

La Hoya Bay Business Village

La Hoya Bay Business Village is the second of a series of projects planned on the magnificent Marjan Island by Khoie Properties. It consists of freehold offices, commercial and retail spaces with a free zone status. La Hoya Bay Business Village will create a modern centre of executive suites that are designed to the highest standards and equipped with the latest technologies, services and superior amenities.

Future Projects

La Hoya Bay Resort, Marina and Yacht Club

Khoie Properties is in negotiation with major international hotel and marina operators in order to establish a 500-room five-star resort, 300-berth marina and a world-class yacht club on this phase.

La Hoya Bay Regency

A residential development set on the beachfront. These serviced units will be finished to an exceptional specification.

La Hoya Bay Pelican

Another residential project, housed within uniquely designed and secure blocks, within a landscaped beachfront setting.

La Hoya Bay Business Hotel

A 250 room 4 star business hotel on a waterfront setting.

Balboa Islands

Khoie Properties has exclusive rights to a further 5.5 million sq ft at the top end of Marjan Island to develop as a master planned residential and commercial community. The project will be an AED 3 billion leisure, business and retail waterfront development.

Khoie Properties
P.O. Box 182398
Dubai,
United Arab Emirates

UAE phone: 800 KHOIE (54643) (Toll free)
Tel: +971 4 33 84 845
Fax: +971 4 33 84 854
Website: www.khoie.com
www.lahoyabay.com

Two of the renowned business houses in the Gulf region - the Al Zahran Group and Al Mahfouz Group entered a joint venture and established **Ishraqah** for Development in July 2006 to leverage on the growth dynamics of the property market, regionally and internationally.

The company has a core focus on buying, selling, developing and investing in property in the UAE and in emerging international markets. Today, Ishraqah has a development portfolio of over AED 6 billion in the UAE with several landmark projects in the pipeline in Saudi Arabia, Morocco, Egypt, India and Pakistan.

Ishraqah is committed to investing in and developing world-class residential and commercial property that meets the needs of cosmopolitan populations and align the company for international expansion. Ishraqah upholds innovative, efficient and transparent business strategies, and is committed to delivering on their promises and providing premium service through a highly professional workforce.

Projects

Seasons Community

Set amidst a self-sustained neighbourhood in Jumeirah Village; The Seasons Community consists of four low-rise clusters reflecting the four seasons of nature through its scrupulous selection of colours. It consists of 1,400 units, four and five bedroom Townhouses, one and two bedroom Apartments and Garden Apartments.

The project offers exceptional amenities such as four swimming pools, two state-of-the-art fitness centres, landscaped gardens, recreational areas, underground parking and 24 hours security.

The Onyx

Standing tall on Sheikh Zayed Road, beside Emaar Business Park, The Onyx consists of two magnificent office buildings and one state-of-the-art business hotel with inspiring amenities. It's built on a total construction area of approximately 237,000 square feet incorporating restaurants and retail facilities.

It offers investors the first freehold corporate opportunity available in the area on Sheikh Zayed Road and will exemplify an open-design concept with magnificent views of The Palm Jumeirah and the Emirates Golf Course.

Ishraqah for Development
P.O.Box 214362, Dubai
United Arab Emirates

Tel: +971 4 3418277
Fax: +971 4 3418797
Email: inquiry@ishraqah.com
Website: www.ishraqah.com

Schön
PROPERTIES

Schön Properties is an established holding company that has several real estate projects in the UAE. Dubai Lagoon, their first project, is an AED 3 billion residential apartment community, located in Dubai Investment Park. With over 6 million sq feet of development area, the apartment community will comprise 49 buildings, consisting of studios 1, 2, and 3 bedroom and penthouse apartments.

Their second project, Schön Business Park, is a USD 200 million state-of-the-art office development, also located in Dubai Investment Park. The ground plus three development which will comprise approximately 410 offices accommodating up to 4,000 employees, has already leased-out 75% since the launch of the project. Located just 5 km from the Jebel Ali Internationa Airport in Dubai Investment Park (DIP), the development spans a built-up area of 1.1 million square feet and provides state-of-the art offices for corporations waiting to relocate near Jebel Ali Free Zone.

Dubai Lagoon - The AED 3 billion Project - Dubai's Single Largest Private Development

A city by itself, 'Dubai Lagoon' is an upcoming property set in the charming, tranquil, and luxurious surroundings of new Dubai. The community is going to be surrounded by five golf courses, two of which are being designed by golf legend Greg Norman and one by Vijay Singh. Conveniently located within the Dubai Investment Park, it is just 15 km away from the upcoming new airport and minutes from two main highways as well as from Dubailand, Dubai Sports City and Dubai Knowledge Village. Dubai Lagoon, the AED 3 billion high watermark of living is spread over an area of 1.75 million sq ft consisting of 51 buildings with nearly 4,104 apartments. This mammoth project which is targeted towards the upper-middle income segment of the society has witnessed a huge demand with phase one comprising 21 buildings being completely sold in a short time span of just 54 days. This rapid success is attributed to the revolutionary 7 years financing plan and also because Dubai Lagoon is the first development project to directly target the middle and upper-middle income demographic segment, previously untapped by other developers.

Schon Properties

Tel: +971 4 3219501
Fax: +971 4 3219507
Toll free: 800 SCHON
Website: www.schonproperties.com

MASTER DEVELOPER

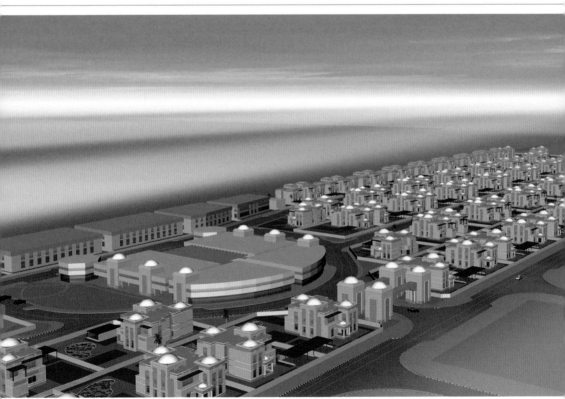

Al Basateen

SNASCO, a UAE based investment and property developer, is a leading firm in the property development sector in the KSA and UAE, with a commitment to the highest standards in its residential, commercial, and industrial development projects.

SNASCO has elaborate plans for further expansion throughout the region, and aims to develop properties with unique architectural and geographical characteristics, which reflect environmental sensitivity, impeccable planning and flawless execution.

The company aims to build up an investment entity with special focus on developing and marketing property projects, seeking new investment opportunities, joining forces with key players in the construction and real estate sectors, and attracting investors and partners.

SNASCO has diversified businesses ranging from investment in land bargains to property studies and investment, and high quality development projects in addition to property selling and marketing and the signing of strategic alliance pacts with leading property firms.

The most prominent of SNASCO's property development projects are the Sharjah Investment Centre and Al Basateen. Its portfolio includes several other large projects in the UAE in addition to future expansion plans.

Al Basateen

Al Basateen is a residential and commercial project located in Al Maliha Street near Sharjah University City. Sprawled on an area of 5.5 million sq m, the project includes 326 plots designated for villas and independent homes, ranging in size from 6,000 square feet to 15,700 square feet, as well as a large mall, entertainment centres, medical care centres and schools, all surrounded by green spaces and parks. This integrated residential and commercial project is located near Sharjah University City which is home to the American University, Sharjah University, Technical Institutes and other educational institutes.

Sharjah Investment Centre

SNASCO Investment and Property Development has already launched the Sharjah Investment Centre (SIC). SNASCO is an investor in this project with other partners, and is its Master Developer. Located on the Emirates Road, a few km away from Sharjah International Airport and Al-Hamriyah Port, SIC stands as a vital, fully integrated, multi-purpose project stretching over 32 million square feet. It features industrial, commercial and residential clusters / compounds and

Sharjah Investment Centre

provides a wide range of logistic and investment services that are likely to significantly strengthen the economic position of Sharjah.

With work commencing on the project a month after its official launch, SNASCO signed a contract with ARABUILCO last December to start flattening works of the project land, demonstrating the firm's commitment to finish works on time, which it has successfully achieved.

SNASCO is the master developer of the Sharjah Investment Centre, and leads a Saudi-Emirate alliance to invest and implement its development. An independent company was founded for this issue under the management and supervision of SNASCO, due to the size of SIC, and to ensure the best uses of its elements, in addition to providing the best management.

The project includes storage areas, labour accommodation, logistic support areas, and a special area for light and medium industry. Additionally there will be hotels, leisure services and a commercial centre, accompanied by the Investment Centre, which will be the first of its kind.

The housing sector provides residential units for all staff levels ranging from managers to labourers, with green passages and entertainment facilities that give tenants a recreational environment after a long day at work. The accommodations are near to the workplaces providing an added convenience for managers and labourers who can now avoid long commutes.

The storage area will have several benefits for manufacturers and businessmen as the SIC is strategically situated on the most important main road in the country, close to Sharjah International Airport and Hamriyah Port.

SIC will stand for the integrated economic and investment environment in the emirate and will have a positive contribution towards a more healthy economic and social situation in Sharjah.

SNASCO Real Estate

Kingdom of Saudi Arabia
P.O.Box 112919, Jeddah 21371
Tel: +966 26927172
Fax: +966 26927585

United Arab Emirates
PO Box: 32595, Sharjah
Tel: +971 6 5751175
Fax: +971 6 5751157

RAK PROPERTIES

An artist's rendering of Mina Al Arab

The United Arab Emirates is viewed as one of the best environments for business and investments in the region. With well-established and modern infrastructure facilities, high quality services, a liberal economic policy and political stability, the UAE has all the pre-requisites for attracting investments and for economic development. The flexibility of economic laws and regulations, in addition to the absence of restrictions on capital movement, tax-free corporate and personal incomes and the 100% ownership of projects, are among the other major factors encouraging enterprise in the Emirates.

One of the emerging emirates providing all these incentives is Ras Al Khaimah (RAK). RAK has become a business destination par excellence with an attractive investment environment and a proactive government keen on encouraging enterprise. In the last two years, the emirate has managed to attract AED 100 billion worth of investments where GDP grew by 13 percent to reach AED 10.4 billion in 2006 and is expected to surge in 2007.

The Government of RAK, under the able guidance of Crown Prince H. H Sheikh Saud bin Saqr Al Qasimi, is serious in its efforts to attract investors to this land of opportunity. The Government is responsive to investor needs and will do everything possible to accommodate serious entrepreneurs who could contribute effectively to the development of the region.

One example of these efforts is the establishment of **RAK Properties**, the premier real estate company in the emirate. It is a Public Joint Stock Company that was formed with the support of the RAK Government to transform RAK into one of the region's leading destinations for tourism and focus on real estate investment.

RAK Properties is a Public Joint Stock Company with a capital of AED 2 billion that was formed with the support of the RAK Government, to transform RAK into one of the region's leading destinations for tourism and real estate investment. The company's founders, including the Government of Ras Al Khaimah, hold 45 per cent of its share capital, while the remaining 55 per cent was distributed in a public offering that was significantly over-subscribed by 57 times.

In February 2006, the company launched its first project, Julfar Towers, a 43-storey twin office and residential project estimated to cost AED 500 million and set for completion in the mid of 2008, followed by Mina Al Arab, spread over 30 million sq ft and with an estimated cost of AED10 billion, in May 2006.

The Julfar Towers consist of two 43-storey towers - one residential, with 349 apartments, and the

Mina Al Arab harbour

RAK Tower

other an office tower with 468 units - built over a three-level podium that provides retail as well as food outlets and central facilities. Perfect for an enjoyable lifestyle and convenient business, Julfar Towers will provide an ultramodern lifestyle of luxury and convenience and much more. Furthermore, investors in the Julfar business tower will enjoy the benefits of 100% foreign ownership.

As for Mina Al Arab, it would be a new waterfront community in Ras Al Khaimah where lush landscaping, protected coastal wetlands and natural pristine beaches come together with homes, hotels and world-class amenities.

Recently, RAK Properties was among the 15 listed companies honoured by the Securities and Commodities Authority for good financial practices and disclosure.

RAK Properties projects also include, RAK Tower in Marina Square. Located in Al Reem Island, Marina Square is a mixed development that will offer a two level shopping arcade, a Cineplex and a marina for yacht-owners. RAK Tower will be one of the many towers forming the Marina Square master plan. RAK Tower will be fully residential tower with different types of apartments and luxurious amenities. It is set to be a RAK Propertie's first project outside the Emirate of Ras Al Khaimah.

RAK Properties
PO Box 31113, Ras Al Khaimah
United Arab Emirates

Tel: +971 7 2284777
Fax: +971 7 2272444

Dubai
Tel: +971 4 3558033
Fax: +9714 3558044
Toll Free: 800 4020

Email: info@rakproperties.net
Website: www.rakproperties.net

146

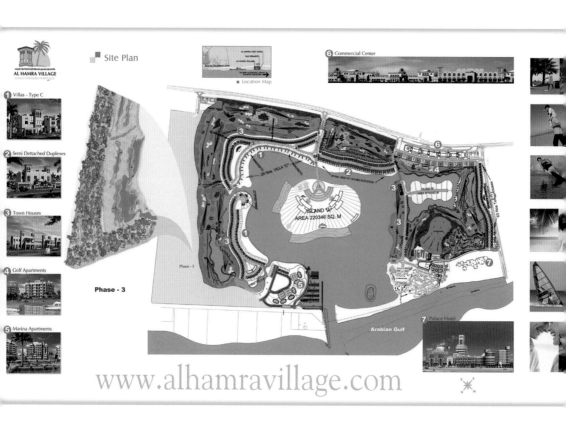

Site Plan

■ Location Map

6 Commercial Center

1 Villas - Type C

2 Semi Dettached Duplexes

3 Town Houses

4 Golf Apartments

5 Marina Apartments

Phase - 3

ISLAND "A"
AREA 220346 SQ. M

7 Palace Hotel

Arabian Gulf

www.alhamravillage.com

Al Hamra Real Estate LLC was created under the guidance of H. H. Sheikh Saud bin Saqr Al Qasimi, the Crown Prince of Ras Al Khaimah. The company is now leading the growth of Ras Al Khaimah with ambitious projects that will propel the emirate onto the world map.

Al Hamra Village

Al Hamra Village's most recently developed project that extends into the Arabian Gulf with a 64 km virgin coastline, is considered a one of a kind endeavour. It is the first 100% freehold development to be built in the emirate of Ras Al Khaimah.

This premium real estate project dubbed as an excellent freehold development property, allows owners a chance to redefine the meaning of luxury living in an integrated and sustainable community.

Lying at the west coast of the United Arab Emirates, the project is set amidst rolling sand dunes against the backdrop of the magnificent Al Hajar Mountains.

The project entails many facilities which make it quite unique. The 5 million square metre expanse is a picturesque sight that is set around salt water lagoons, with a championship golf course and its own marina.

The seaside commercial cum residential resort, is being built in 3 phases. The first phase, which is 100% sold-out, will have 3-bedroom townhouses and 4-bedroom semi-detached duplexes.

The second phase, also 100% sold, will cover the development of additional 3-bedroom townhouses, studios and 1-bedroom golf apartments, 5-bedroom villas (Villa B), 6-bedroom villas (Villa C), studio to 3-bedroom marina apartments, and the first 9 holes of the golf course.

Al Hamra Village already contains the Al Hamra Fort Hotel, but will also contain the 22-floor, 400-room, 5-star, 116 metre (380 foot) Al Hamra Palace Hotel. Another hotel will be built on the 2.3 million square foot (214 thousand square metres) man-made island that will be linked to the rest of the Al Hamra Village project by a bridge.

There will be other sub-development projects such as the Royal Breeze - one of the seven Arabian heritage style 7-storey buildings, completed towards the end of 2007, about 200 metres from the unspoiled private beach.

Different Villa Types, Al Hamra Village, Ras Al Khaimah

World-class amenities and facilities include boutiques, hotels and restaurants, an 18-hole golf course, private beaches, water sports, the latest telecommunication facilities and state-of-the-art security on site.

Al Hamra Real Estate LLC
PO Box 4714, Ras Al Khaimah
United Arab Emirates

Tel: +971 7 2445046
Fax: +971 7 2445270
Email: info@alhamravillage.com
Website: www.alhamravillage.com

MINA AL FAJER

Offering the discerning homeowner a unique lifestyle community, Mina Al Fajer Resort is a ground breaking development situated in the picturesque emirate of Fujairah. Located at the foot of the Hajar Mountains, the 777,025 sq ft mixed-use project is the brainchild of **Mina Al Fajer Real Estate LLC** a leading property development firm specializing in quality projects and luxurious resorts developed to the highest international standards. With His Highness Dr. Sheikh Sultan bin Khalifa bin Zayed Al Nahyan as chairman, the company is looking at diversifying its portfolio of leading real estate developments to the entire Middle East, across Europe and the Indian Ocean.

Mina Al Fajer Resort

Location: Fujairah; at the base of the Hajar mountains, on the Indian Ocean
777,025 sq ft mixed-use development housing luxury residential, hotel facilities, spa, sports amenities, parks and retail.

The Development comprises:
- The Marina
- The Marina Apartments
- The Mountain Villas
- The Solarium Villas
- The Fairmont Hotel

The Marina (100 berths)
- Restaurants
- Boardwalks
- Shopping

The Marina Apartments (70 apartments)
- 2, 3 or 4 bedroom apartments/duplex units
- Interior: state-of-the art technology with designer finishes
- Exterior: landscaped parks/gardens, marina views
- 10 retail outlets

The Apartments
- 2 bedroom: 5 types, floor area ranging from 153.34 – 247.07 sq m
- 3 bedroom: 2 types, floor area ranging from 220 – 245 sq m

Mina Al Fajer

Duplex
- 2 bedroom: 2 types, floor area ranging from 175 – 192 sq m
- 4 bedroom: 1 type, floor area ranging from 264 – 273 sq m

The Mountain Villas (48 villas)
- View of Hajar Mountains and Indian Ocean
- Options include private courtyards, manicured gardens and private pool

Solarium Villas (13 villas)
- 2 storey luxury villas
- Located at the foot of the Hajar Mountains
- Eastern exposure ensuring view of sunrise year-round

The Fairmont Hotel
- 5 star luxury
- More than 200 rooms
- Amenities include: on-site restaurant, spa, health club and pool bar

Mina Al Fajer Real Estate LLC

Dubai Office:
Fairmont Hotel, 2nd Floor
P.O.Box 122373, Dubai
United Arab Emirates

Tel: + 971 4 3322117
Fax: +971 4 3311868

Fujairah Office:
Dibba Main Road

Tel: +971 9 2440660
Fax: +971 9 2440606

Email: info@minaalfajer.ae
Website: www.minaalfajer.ae

Abraj Property Developers
Tel: +971 4 3377977
Fax: +971 4 3377855
Website: www.abrajdubai.com

Abyaar Real Estate Developers
Tel: +971 4 3437727
Fax: +971 4 3437883
Website: www.abyaar.com

ACI Real Estate
Tel: +971 4 3949049
Fax: +971 4 3954744
Website: www.aci-dubai.net

Arenco Real Estate
Tel: +971 4 3372402
Fax: +971 4 3375335
Website: www.arencore.com

Armada Group
Tel: +971 4 3317222
Fax: +971 4 3316565
Website: www.armadaholding.com

Aspire
Tel: +971 4 3390123
Fax: +971 4 3390164
Website: www.aspiredubai.com

Ajman Holding
Toll Free: 800 264
Website: www.ajmanholding.ae

Aldar Properties PJSC
Tel: +971 2 6964444
Fax: +971 2 6417501
Website: www.aldar.com

Al Barari Development LLC
Tel: +971 4 3446855
Fax: +971 4 3422088
Website: www.albarari.com

Al Fajer Properties LLC
Tel: +971 4 3300633
Fax: +971 4 3300611
Website: www.alfajerproperties.ae

Al Faraa' Properties
Tel: +971 4 3961118
Fax: +971 4 3964448
Website: www.alfaraaproperties.com

Al Hamra Real Estate
Tel: +971 7 2445046
Fax: +971 7 2445270
Website: www.alhamravillage.com

Al Kaheel
Tel: +971 4 3411119
Fax: +971 4 3411444
Website: www.alkaheel.com

Al Mazaya Plaza Real Estate
Tel: +971 4 3621110
Fax: +971 4 3621109
Website: www.mazayarealestate.com

Al Maskan Real Estate
Tel: +971 4 3522122
Fax: +971 4 3520333
Website: www.almaskan.com

Al Qudra Holding
Tel: +971 2 6992222
Fax: +971 2 6765500
Website: www.alqudraholding.ae

B&M FZCO
Tel: +971 4 2996968
Fax: +971 4 2996965
Email: b_mdubai@emirates.net.ae
Website: www.bmriviera.com

Bonyan International Investment Group LLC
Tel: +971 4 2296222
Fax: +971 4 2296226
Website: www.boyangroup.com

Burooj Properties LLC
Tel: +971 2 6100100
Fax: +971 2 6673698
Website: www.burooj.ae

City of Arabia
Tel: +971 4 3311022
Fax: +971 4 3322334
Website: www.cityofarabia.ae

Damac Holding
Tel: +971 4 3322005
Fax: +971 4 3325355
Website: www.damacproperties.com

Deyaar Development PJSC
Tel: +971 4 2955844
Toll free: 800-339227
Fax: +971 4 2957711
Website: www.deyaar.ae

Dheeraj & East Coast
Tel: +971 4 3417333
Fax: +971 4 3417373
Website: www.dheerajeastcoast.com

Dubai International Properties
Tel: +971 4 3300055
Fax: +971 4 3304466
Website: www.sama-dubai.com

Dubailand
Tel: +971 4 3680000
Fax: +971 4 3681111
Website: www.dubailand.ae

Dubai Properties
Tel: +971 4 3911114
Fax: +971 4 3695300
Website: www.dubai-properties.ae

Dubai Sports City
Tel: +971 4 3293300
Fax: +971 4 3293388
Website: www.dubaisportscity.ae / www.sc.ae

Emaar
Tel: +971 4 3673333
Fax: +971 4 3673000
Website: www.emaar.ae

ETA Star Property Developers LLC
Tel: +971 4 2687222 / 800 827827
Fax: +971 4 2623291
Website: www.etastar.com

Falak Properties
Tel: +971 4 3441100
Fax: +971 4 3441110
Website: www.falakproperties.com

Fortune Group
Tel: +971 4 3316789
Fax: +971 4 3318118
Website: www.fortunegroup.ae

Falcon City of Wonders LLC
Tel: +971 4 3355539
Fax: +971 4 3356703
Website: www.falconcity.com

High Rise LLC
Tel: +971 4 3212120
Fax: +971 4 3212128
Website: www.highrise.ae

Hydra Properties
Tel: +971 4 2294499
Fax: +971 4 2294447
Website: www.hydraproperties.com

Ishraqah for Development Ltd.
Tel: +971 4 3418277
Fax: +971 4 3418797
Website: www.ishraqah.com

IRIS
Tel: +971 4 3344115
Fax: +971 4 3344457
Website: www.iris.ae

Khoie Properties
Tel: +971 4 3384845
Fax: +971 4 3384854
Email: info@khoie.com
Website: www.khoie.com

KM Properties
Tel: +971 4 2951615
Fax: +971 4 2951484
Email: kmp@km-properties.com
Website: www.km-properties.com

Limitless LLC
Tel: +971 4 3601818
Fax: +971 4 3601819
Website: www.limitless.ae

Madison Holdings FZ Co
Tel: +971 4 351 9922
Fax: +971 4 3519944
Website: www.madison-holdings.net

MAG Properties
Tel: +971 4 3353301
Fax: +971 4 3353033
Website: www.magpd.com

Mina Al Fajer
Tel: +971 4 3322117
Fax: +971 4 3311868
Website: www.minaalfajer.ae

Mizin
Toll Free: 800 (MIZIN) 64946
Fax: +971 4 4250266
Website: www.mizin.ae

Nakheel
Tel: +971 4 3903333
Fax: +971 4 3903314
Website: www.nakheel.com

Omniyat Properties
Tel: +971 4 3063300
Fax: +971 4 3063333
Website: www.omniyat.com

RAK Properties
Tel: +971 7 2284777
Fax: +971 7 2272444
Website: www.rakproperties.net

Rais Developers LLC
Tel: +971 4 3218800
Fax: +971 4 3218822
Website: www.rasis.ae

Reem Investments
Tel: +971 2 6444455
Fax: +971 2 6444463
Website: www.reemi.ae

Reef Real Estate Investment Co.LLC
Tel: +971 4 3293330
Fax: +971 4 3293331
Website: www.reefrealestate.net

Sama Dubai
Tel: +971 4 3300055
Fax: +971 4 3304466
Website: www.sama-dubai.com

Schön Properties
Tel: +971 4 3219501
Toll free: 800 72466
Fax: +971 4 3219507
Website: www.schonproperties.com

Shaikh Holdings
Tel: +971 4 3642722
Fax: +971 4 3678054
Email: info@shaikh-holdings.com
Website: www.shaikh-holdings.com

SNASCO
Tel: +971 6 5751175
Fax: +971 6 5751157
Email: info@snasco.com
Website: www.snasco.com

Sorouh
Tel: +971 2 4440006
Fax: +971 2 4440066
Email: sales@sorouh.com
Website: www.sorouh.com

Silicon Gates
Tel: +971 4 2940504
Fax: +971 4 2940603
Email: info@silicongatesdubai.com
Website: www.silicongatesdubai.com

Tameer
Tel: +971 6 5995000
Fax: +971 6 5775722
Email: info@tameer.net
Website: www.tameer.net

Tanmiyat Group
Tel: +971 4 3329110
Fax: +971 4 3329115
Email: info@tanmiyat.com
Website: www.tanmiyat.com

Tatweer
Tel: +971 4 3302222
Fax: +971 4 3302010
Website: www.tatweerdubai.com

Trident International Holdings
Tel: +971 4 8830555
Fax: +971 4 8830808
Website: www.tihglobal.com

Union Properties
Tel: +971 4 8851555
Fax: +971 4 8852666
Website: www.up.ae

Wind Properties
Tel: +971 4 2274973
Fax: +971 4 2246378
Email: firozeh@windproperties.com
Website: www.windproperties.com

You've always been moved by German standards.
Now, welcome home to the same.

A Property is much more than an investment. It's home to someone's lifelong dreams.
Which is why, Bavaria Gulf invests its projects with uncompromising quality and attention to every detail.
A leader in residential projects in Germany, the name brings with it a brand new dimension
of 'Total Quality Assurance' to the real estate market of the region.

BAVARIA GULF
GERMAN PRECISION MEETS GOOD LIVING

Project Development • Acquisition & Consulting • Property & Facility Management • Sales & Leasing

Bavaria Gulf Real Estate L.L.C., Office No: 1308, Grosvenor House Commercial Tower,
Sheikh Zayed Road, P.O. Box 214970, Dubai, United Arab Emirates. Tel: +971 4 329 88 80 Fax: +971 4 329 88 13
www.bavaria-gulf.com

Real Estate Agents and Secondary Market

Whether you are overseas and looking for property investment opportunities, or you are currently living in the UAE and thinking about buying a home or a buy-to-let property in Abu Dhabi, **LLJ Property** can help you. As Abu Dhabi's leading real estate agency LLJ Property provides a personal, tailor made, professional service to guide you through the purchase process.

LLJ Property was established in 2005, to meet the needs of the emerging Abu Dhabi real estate market. The Abu Dhabi based founding partners have over 30 years of combined property experience in the UAE and an extensive and unmatched knowledge of the Abu Dhabi real estate sector.

An established track record as highly regarded industry professionals has led to LLJ Property becoming one of the estate agents of choice in Abu Dhabi. The company offers a comprehensive schedule of property services including:

Property Sales - The multilingual sales team has a reputation for high quality customer care. They are experienced in handling sales of off-plan property, for both local and foreign individual and bulk purchasers. LLJ Property's international division primarily focuses on the sale of investment property located in the UK.

Property Leasing – LLJ Property offers full leasing management service to residential and commercial landlords. The leasing team has a reputation for understanding and responding effectively to individual and corporate clients seeking residential, commercial or retail space to lease.

Property Management - To cater for the growing Abu Dhabi property ownership market, LLJ Property has developed bespoke Property Management systems to specifically suit the UAE. These systems cater for both portfolio and individual owners, providing a complete solution for both residential and commercial landlords.

The Abu Dhabi Real Estate Market

Why Abu Dhabi?
Abu Dhabi is the capital city of the UAE and is currently experiencing phenomenal economic growth as it becomes one of the region's foremost financial and cultural centres.
The emerging Abu Dhabi real estate market with current projects valued at USD 270 billion (AED 992 billion) is a key driver of this growth. Some other key economic facts to consider are:
* 8.2% rise in GDP in 2007 with a projected rise to USD159 billion by 2010
* Phenomenal increase of foreign direct investment exceeding USD 160 billion in the real estate sector

- Tax free haven for residents and businesses
- USD 10 billion port redevelopment and USD 3 billion investment in industrial clusters will attract major international manufacturers, commercial centres and businesses
- Tourism sector growing 17% annually
- Etihad Airways is scheduled to fly to over 70 international destinations by 2010

Abu Dhabi is also attracting international organisations and events in its aim to create a major cultural destination. The city will be home to the largest **Guggenheim Museum** in the world and the first **Louvre Museum** outside Paris. It is also the latest destination on the Formula One Grand Prix Circuit and will host the regions first and world's largest Warner Brothers Theme Park.

The real estate sector is still relatively young but has already announced multi billion dollar development projects to create much needed additional residential and commercial space for the rapidly growing city. Analysts have predicted that this market will overtake others in the region and that demand for residential property will continue to rise.

Abu Dhabi's population is projected to double in the next decade driving demand for residential and commercial development. Both office and residential properties have increased in value and rental rates in prime areas have jumped by up to 50%. Forecasters envisage 'rents will stay on a rising curve, while capital values will be underpinned by high and rising demand.' *Business News Jan 2007*.

The government is ensuring that developers phase property releases and carefully plan construction to allow the market to keep pace and avoid oversupply. There is also a commitment to developing infrastructure first so that current journey times within the city are minimally effected by construction.

Leading real estate financers are buoyant in their predictions about the market expecting residential retail real estate sales in Abu Dhabi to reach around USD 2.5 billion (AED 9.2 billion) in 2007, with a mortgage market valued at more than USD 800 million (AED 2.9 billion) by the end of the year.

Abu Dhabi Property Law
The Abu Dhabi Property Law passed in August 2005 by UAE President and Ruler of Abu Dhabi, H.H. Sheikh Khalifa bin Zayed Al Nahyan currently allows UAE nationals to own and trade land, GCC citizens to do so within designated Investment Areas and other expatriates to invest within the Investment Areas.

Investment Areas
An Investment Area is an area designated by the relevant Abu Dhabi authorities as suitable for the development of property for sale to all nationalities. Current identified Investment Areas are

Reem Island and Al Raha Beach with more likely to be announced in the near future.

Reem Island is a 633 hectare natural island located 300m off the North East Coast of Abu Dhabi Island. It is home to projects from three master developers, Shams Abu Dhabi by Sorouh Real Estate, City of Lights and Marina Square from Tamouh Investments and Najmat Abu Dhabi by Reem Investments.

Al Raha Beach is 500 hectares of waterfront land adjacent to the Abu Dhabi - Dubai highway which will be developed into 11 distinct precincts by master developer Aldar Properties.

Finding the Right Property

Meet with a reputable real estate company with relevant local market experience to discuss the pros and cons of various options.

Compare the costs of property per square foot and also individual unit costs. Often an efficient, well designed unit can be a better buy than a larger poorly designed one.

Consider why you are buying? Is it for rental or personal use?
If rental, consider who your potential tenant will be and what they will require. Try to be objective and remove any personal 'must haves' as you won't be living in it.
Factor in buying and selling costs and any fees associated with ownership and the management of the property. If it is an investment property, calculate potential rental yield. Look at current rents in as similar a unit as possible, taking into consideration location, size and facilities.

Financial Considerations

Financing is available from different lenders depending on the project and individual circumstances. It is recommended that you confirm finance before committing yourself. There will be associated costs with buying property including but not limited to registration and transfer fees, maintenance and service charges.

For more information on property for sale or lease in Abu Dhabi, contact:

LLJ Property LLC
PO Box 107729, Abu Dhabi, United Arab Emirates
Tel: +971 2 6274110
Toll Free: 800 Call LLJ (800 2255 555)
Fax: + 971 2 6274112
Email: admin@lljproperty.com
Website: www.lljproperty.com

betterhomes

Founded in 1986, **Better Homes**, Dubai's largest and most reputed real estate agency is at the forefront of the property boom in the Emirate. As a founding member of the Dubai Property Group, striving to improve and regulate the property market in Dubai, and with over 20 years of invaluable market experience, Better Homes has the best selection of property in the region; selling, leasing, and managing more properties than any other agency in the Gulf. Employing over 400 staff and the only certified property consultants in Dubai, the company's formula for success is simple: better people, better ideas and better properties.

Aiming to take the 'pain' out of property and provide an easier, more enjoyable customer experience, Better Homes offers many services that are a market first. Specialist services such as Project Sales & Marketing, Short-term Rentals, and Property Management are all examples of how Better Homes sets the standard for others to follow.

In a marketplace plagued with a pressure-oriented sales style, Better Homes' attitude towards real estate is friendly and refreshing. The company has several relaxing and stylishly designed boutiques throughout Dubai that are a stark contrast to the confining and cramped real estate offices commonplace in the region. In line with its friendly personality, Better Homes realises how important it is for a client to be in a comfortable environment to facilitate the right property decision. The company's two publications, Better Living and Property Listings provide readers with user friendly guides on living in Dubai and choosing the most suitable property.

With customer service at the core of their philosophy and the real estate industry's most advanced IT system; Better Homes' specialist software gives clients exclusive features like the most up-to-the-minute properties available and interactive online maps. Developers can view projected unit mixes and returns, whilst landlords receive 24 hour online access to everything that's happening with their property. At Better Homes, they make the best of cutting-edge technology to give you cutting-edge service.

The company has expanded its range of services to include the following divisions: Sales, Leasing, Short-term Rentals, Property Management, Commercial Advisory, Project Sales & Marketing, Engineering and Interiors. Better Homes continues to go from strength to strength with expansion into new international markets such as Europe, Asia, and the Middle East.

Despite this remarkable growth, Better Homes has never outgrown its philosophy of providing the most trustworthy and personalised service around. From Dubai to London to Mumbai, people are discovering the benefits of a better property experience.

Sales

With a wide international network, sellers can benefit from unrivalled global exposure whilst buyers can enjoy unrivalled choice. Along with helpful financial and legal advice, why go anywhere else?

Leasing

Fully personalised services are available to both landlords and tenants to meet their individual requirements. Tenants are matched to a suitable property from an extensive database while landlords can rest assured their property is being exposed to deliver optimum occupancy and maximum returns.

Short-term Rentals

Offering readymade, short-term living solutions for when you are on business, on holiday or in Dubai for an interim period. With a wide range of luxurious and quality properties to chose from, short-term rentals is guaranteed to find you a place to call home.

Property Management

Acting on behalf of landlords, a complete facility and tenant management service is provided. From maintenance and lease management through to legal and financial advice, Better Homes ensures that your property is optimized and retains its competitive edge.

Commercial Advisory

Putting your business first is easier than before thanks to an extensive range of commercial properties for sale and lease. Whether looking for office, retails, warehouse, labour camp or land and buildings, Better Homes has got a suitable and cost effective solution for you.

Project Sales and Marketing

Better Homes offer specialised sales and marketing services an select clients with prestigious developments. From developing a unique selling point to formulating pricing strategies and achieving the right unit size and mix, the team has the expertise to make your development a runaway success.

Engineering

Providing quality and cost-effective property care, is a dedicated facilities management service that looks after your technical and infrastructure requirements.

The engineering team strives to protect the longevity of your property.

Interiors

Better Homes offer decorating solutions for all tastes, styles and budgets with tailor made solutions for your home. From curtains to carpets to accessories – get the best materials for the best value, saving you time and money along the way while making sure your home looks exactly the way you want it.

Perils and Positives of buying in the secondary market

Let the buyer beware.

First and foremost, buyers would be well advised to deal only with a reputable real estate company registered with the Dubai Property Group. There are a few pitfalls that the buyer needs to be aware of.

The surge in real estate construction is a global issue that has impacted on the real estate market in the UAE. The lack of market indicators, such as average house prices, makes an assessment of the UAE property difficult.

The absence of real estate price inflation makes the rise in Dubai property prices distinctive. Investors purchasing property to sell on the secondary market or lease have been the main purchasers, but end user purchasers are now on the increase. This is likely to impact the level of supply on the secondary market in the future.

Dubai's economy is growing strongly across all sectors and holiday makers purchasing a second home are an important driver for the real estate market. It is fair to say that Dubai's real estate boom still has some way to go. The level of projected real estate investment alone will support robust economic growth over the medium term. Previously, some non registered real estate companies would try to capitalise on the market conditions by advertising the properties at a previously quoted price to attract investors, thereby misleading the buyer and damaging the credibility of the real estate market. However, since the establishment of the Real Estate Regulatory Authority (RERA), agencies have to be registered and such incidents should reduce. A credible agent will be able to advise investors on the current market value of properties and the likely return on investment on any particular development projects.

Established in 1986, Better Homes is one of the founding members of the Dubai Property Group and has been instrumental in the continued improvement and regulation of the Dubai property market over the years.

The Sale and Purchase Agreement

There are three important factors that should be in any contract:

• The Parties, (Buyer and Seller)

• The Property

• The Price

The terms of payment should be outlined including amounts and timelines of payments. Any restrictive conditions should be added e.g. if the sale is subject to the buyer obtaining finance etc. Most forms of property purchase agreement acknowledge not only the need for the buyer to become the registered owner of the freehold – but also the possibility of the buyer financing the transaction by way of a mortgage. In some agreements the ownership changes hands from the developer to the buyer only once the purchase price has been paid in full. When dealing with a reputable real estate firm, such as Better Homes, the agency will hold the money for the purchaser on behalf of the seller until the transfer date. If monies are to be paid over to the seller for any reason, the purchaser will be informed and will be given the relevant guarantees.

The Secondary Market

What are the procedures in order to sell one's property on the secondary market? Each developer may have different requirements, and it is advisable to check with the agent and/or the developer before considering selling on the secondary market. The most basic requirements are that the seller lists the property with an agency and issues proof of ownership, thereby entering into an agreement with the agency.

Financing

Until recently many expatriate homeowners interested in investing in Dubai property boom may have considered re-mortgaging their homes in order to raise the funds to invest. In the past, Dubai mortgages were difficult to obtain and expensive, leaving no option for financing but equity release. Until very recently, mortgages were only offered by the major developers in conjunction with domestic lenders because the real estate market was relatively immature and legislation was not in place to legalise foreigners' right to buy freehold title in Dubai.

However, recent legislative developments have resulted in the major banks and finance houses cashing in on the property boom. Global names in banking are now offering customers mortgage facilities to buy residential and buy-to-let accommodation. In the longer term, this is expected to result in greater competition in the pricing of mortgage products and interest rates.

The role of the Facilitator

How does the facilitator make a difference?

Having a representative who is concerned about your interests is very important. The client pays the real estate agent and therefore will be looked after. Again it is important to choose a reputable agent and to take care in reviewing all the documents you are requested to sign. Don't hand over any funds until you are sure of your position – and make sure you have an agreement and a receipt. If in doubt, you may want to seek legal advice.

A facilitator such as Better Homes' role is consultative. They assess your requirements to narrow down your choices and make recommendations. Below are common terms and issues to consider when purchasing a property:

- **Buying a property – the first things to consider**
  Decide on a budget, secure financing, and then choose a property. Explore real estate websites and the property pages of The Gulf News to get an idea of what is available in the market.

- **Finance options available**
  Various options are available from several financial institutions. Interest rates vary from between 6% and 11.5%. (Please see section on Financial Institutions.)

- **Buying to let**
  You can buy a property and then rent it out in the UAE. Better Homes can help you with these arrangements. We also have a leasing and property management division. Our interiors division can assist you with furnishing your home.

- **Where to buy in the UAE**
  Non-UAE nationals can only buy in areas designated specifically for expatriate freehold and leasehold sales (please see section on Property Developers)

- **Visa requirements for purchasing property**
  You do not need to be a UAE resident to purchase property in the UAE. You become eligible to apply for a residence visa upon the purchase of a freehold property. (Please note that the usual immigration laws apply to all residency applications; the purchase of a property does not guarantee a residence visa.)

- **Anticipated premiums on the resale of property**
  Re-sale values are difficult to predict, and vary depending on type of property and location of the same but a reputable real estate agent would be able to advise on likely premiums, based on current market conditions.

- **Yearly appreciation of property values**
  There are two segments of the market - the segment open to all buyers and the segment that is open to UAE nationals only. The "open-to-all nationalities" segment is still in its infancy stage, therefore, no definitive data is available.

- **Projected appreciation values**

  It is difficult to project the appreciation values, as the market is so new. However, market analysts are confident that when the market stabilises, property in Dubai will represent a good investment in the long term.

- **The 'base price'**

  The base price is the price at which the developer released the property for sale initially.

- **The 'selling price'**

  The selling price is the price at which the property is currently on the market.

- **The 'premium'**

  The premium is the difference between the base price and the selling price. In other words, the initial investor's profit.

- **Registration Fee to the Lands Department**

  The registration fee of 1.5% to the Lands Department is applicable to all property types. The buyer pays this.

- **Other costs to consider**

  Other purchasing costs may include a transfer fee to the developer of resale properties. This is usually between 1% and 7% (depending on the development) of the base price of the property.

Pitfalls to consider while buying property

Pitfall 1

Advertised properties that have already been sold or increased prices. Always check that the advertising agent is registered with the Dubai Property Group, and ask to have details of properties sent to you with current asking prices.

Pitfall 2

No keys available when viewing properties. Often unfinished properties cannot be viewed, as developers will not give keys to owners till handover.

Pitfall 3

Description of the property is misleading or incorrect. Unless you are buying off-plan, you can visit the property yourself and take measurements. Always take the description of the property with you to compare with the real thing.

Pitfall 4

Agents' or Developers' representative being late for appointments or not even arriving. A reputable agent will respect their clients' time and will arrive promptly, or call ahead if there are any problems.

Pitfall 5

Number of rooms/size misrepresented in the adverts. Again, always take the description of the property with you, and be prepared with a tape measure!

Pitfall 6

Telephone calls are not returned. This is very common in all aspects of business in Dubai. One way to avoid this is to ask to be connected to the voicemail of the person you are contacting, or ask when they will be available and offer to ring again at a convenient time. Reputable agents will respect your patience and endeavour to get back to you at the earliest possible opportunity.

Pitfall 7

Cash payments are risky. Always ensure that you have a signed copy of your contract and ask for a receipt. Always read the fine print carefully before entering into a cash agreement.

Pitfall 8

All Inclusive Price is seldom quoted. Check this with your agent and ask for the quoted price (including breakdown) in writing.

Pitfall 9

Delay in transfer as one of the parties is out of town. Delay in transfer can prejudice a buyer, as the seller can change his mind or sell the property for a higher price. Make sure that you factor delays into your agreement and communicate this with the seller, and include this in your contract as well.

Better Homes
P.O. Box 29726, Dubai
United Arab Emirates

Tel: +971 4 3447714
Website: www.bhomes.com

DUBAI
LUXURY HOMES
COMMERCIAL · RESIDENTIAL · INVESTMENT

When it comes to finding the ideal property in Dubai, you may well shudder at the thought of picking up one of the property pages which are distributed with the local broadsheets. Whether you are purchasing your first home or you want to take advantage of the investment opportunities that are currently present in the industry, trawling through supplements that are jam packed with hundreds of agents vying for attention, could well end up dissuading rather than encouraging one to invest. How can too much choice be a bad thing, you ask? When it starts to confuse, rather than clarify, is the answer.

This is where **Luxury Homes LLC** comes in. We are a British-run real estate brokerage licensed by the Dubai Department of Economic Development and also registered with the Lands Department to carry out real estate broking and other property related activities. Formed in 2003 with the goal of providing an unrivalled professional and personal service both for local and overseas residents who wish to invest in Gulf based property. So be it buying, selling, renting, or leasing a property in Dubai or Abu Dhabi, and whether you're interested in residential or commercial properties, Luxury Homes LLC can provide you with a level of service of the highest possible standard.

Our comprehensive core service range includes:
- Impartial advice on 'off plan' purchases, both residential and commercial
- Step by step assistance in purchasing secondary market properties
- Property sales for both individual and corporate clients
- Investment advice for property investors
- Property rentals, working with landlords and tenants
- Professional property management services
- Professional relocation services

'Off Plan' Purchases
Purchasing 'off plan' property, sometimes before there is even any physical evidence of a building, remains extremely popular in Dubai and investors still have to choose whether to purchase directly from developers or seek independent advice. Taking into account key considerations such as availability of finance, location, completion dates etc. we are able to ensure the right decisions are made in all situations. The experience and expertise of the Luxury Homes staff, who have been involved with 'off plan' purchases since they were first introduced in Dubai, make them ideally placed to advise.

Secondary Market Purchases
Our staff have access to up-to-the-minute information on available Dubai properties and maintain a comprehensive database, and this coupled with excellent local knowledge of the Dubai property market puts them in a position to give guidance and impartial advice to the client

whether they require a residential or an investment property.

Individual and Corporate Clients

Both categories are catered for at Luxury Homes LLC. Whether it's taking the time to finding exactly the individual home to meet the client's requirements or a larger project for a corporate buyer, staff will ensure that specific needs are met and that a consultant with experience and expertise within the required area is assigned to the customer.

Property Rentals

In such a fast moving market it is important for landlords to have the ability of quickly sourcing tenants and that tenants are able to secure the right residential or commercial property. The Luxury Homes rental department has a growing database of property to rent in all of the most popular areas. In addition, we have a well established network of contacts that can assist with the property search.

Professional Property Management Services

Our property management services are aimed at meeting the needs of private investors and corporate clients alike. From well structured packaged services at different levels to tailor made solutions, our management services are highly flexible. Professional property management helps to ensure that the interests of the investor are protected and the tenant has a trouble free tenancy.

Professional Relocation Services

Emigrating to a new country can be a complicated and stressful process. There are many things one has to consider, whether this is what schools are available to your children or how easy it is to organize international shipping. Luxury Homes combine excellent local knowledge with professional expertise to provide a bespoke service to anyone who is planning to immigrate to Dubai.

Luxury Homes Ethos

The team at Luxury Homes LLC pride themselves on an ethical and transparent approach to business, only recommending what we believe will be appropriate for individual needs. As a result of this honesty, transparency and impartiality, clients are happy to come back to us time and time again and frequently refer their friends and business acquaintances to us safe in the knowledge of our integrity. The multinational staff are individually profiled on our website.

Industry News

Since the formation of the company in 2003, we have been following our own set of strict procedures and rules, endeavouring to build a reputation as honest and straightforward. We now welcome the formation of the Real Estate Regulatory Authority (RERA) and the stability it will bring to the industry. The introduction of a formal governing body with the ability to pass and amend laws is sure to bring peace of mind to developers, investors, landlords and agents alike. The property market in Dubai may well still be referred to as just out of infancy, but with the introduction of the RERA, it can certainly be said to have matured dramatically.

Dubai Luxury Homes

Tel: +971 4 3039300
Fax: +971 4 3039301

Email: info@dubailuxuryhomes.com
Website: www.dubailuxuryhomes.com

Engel & Völkers specializes in acting as agent for premium residential and commercial properties. Founded 30 years ago the company concentrated on the sale of high-class residential real estate in the Hamburg suburbs along the Elbe River. Over the years Engel & Völkers has grown into the largest German property agency and now is one of the world's leading real estate service companies, represented in 22 countries spanning over four continents.

The success of the company is based on a partner system in which self-employed entrepreneurs around the globe are becoming a part of. The Group's revenues are growing in line with this, at global, two-figure percentage rates. In 2006, the Group sold property with a total value of approximately two billion euros and the revenue figures of the Engel & Völkers brand exceeded 100 million euros.

Engel & Völkers combined its experience in Real Estate with innovative ideas and set foot into the United Arab Emirates and the Middle East in 2004. Since then Engel & Völkers opened four shops in Dubai and one in Abu Dhabi and is looking forward to expand throughout the Middle East.

Engel & Völkers has laid the basis for a strong brand with clearly defined services and a strong focus on selected property markets. In addition to the group's activities as agents, the services also comprise in-depth consulting services for our customers in regards to the sale and purchase of residential and commercial properties, rental, management as well as strategic development and optimization of existing portfolios.

Services

Sales: The decision to buy or sell a property is a matter of trust. That is why such an important decision should be placed in the hands of an experienced service provider, who will give you optimal guidance and attain the best possible result for you. Engel & Völkers combine the capabilities of a competent team with a world-wide network. Their strength is based on the in-depth training of employees, on constantly updated information and on continuous knowledge transfer within the company.

Leasing: Whether you are renting a villa, apartment, town home, or any other rental; you receive guaranteed leads from an extensive network. The company also has commercial properties under their portfolio.

Short Term Rentals: Management service contracts are tailored to suit your needs and that of your tenants. Luxury furnished flats for short term rentals are centrally located in the best districts and offer convenience and comfort beyond the common hotel rooms.

178

Property Management: Engel & Völkers provide clients with value added services that surpass their expectations and requirements. They use their expertise and knowledge to maximize returns with minimal effort. Amongst the services offered are several packages to suit client needs while keeping in mind the importance of competent and cost effective management.

As a part of the Engel & Völkers franchisees all employees can access a global network comprising approximately 223 residential and commercial properties at any time. Qualified cross-selling is an essential foundation for the growing success of the company. Numerous investors and businesses are expanding abroad and let their branch offices be managed exclusively by their network – another field of activities for the highly qualified franchisees.

Engel & Völkers combine the capabilities of a highly competent team with a world-wide network. Their strength is based on the in-depth training of employees with high-level vocational and further professional training by the means of the **Engel & Völkers Property Academy** which was founded in 1996. The Property Academy is proficiently managed by trainers with several years' experience and is continually adapting to both the needs of the company's internal systems and the property market.

The in house publication **Grund Genug (Global Guide)** ia used to advertise exclusive properties under the Engel & Völkers portfolio. Grund Genug is a high profile architecture and lifestyle magazine that was first issued in 1989. It is published quarterly and distributed with 70,000 copies in German, English and Spanish and has defined architectural and design trends, providing tips to potential buyers worldwide and presenting exhaustive reports and stories about homes and lifestyles.

Whether you want to rent or let, buy or sell, invest or develop a project – whether it's a matter of acquiring land or a turnkey property, renovation or new construction, apartment, mansion or holiday home – Engel & Völkers portfolio is extensive and high class.

Engel & Völkers corporate vision is not to follow, but to lead and provide end-to-end real estate solutions for each individual client to satisfy their every need and therefore to ensure highest client satisfaction. Discretion as well as protecting the interests of the customers is a point of honour. Ultimately the brand's success is also due to these values. Engel & Völkers firmly counts on innovation and co-operation, professionalism and reliability.

ENGEL & VÖLKERS
Dubai Emarat, Zentrum Real Estate Brokers LLC
License partner of ENGEL &VÖLKERS Medaville Middle East Ltd.
P.O.Box 28 29 23 , Dubai, United Arab Emirates
Tel: +971 4 3388104 Fax: +971 4 3388105
Website: www.engelvoelkers.com/dubaiemarat

eqarat.com is more than a company. They are an ambitiously innovative real estate philosophy, at the vanguard of revolutionizing the staggeringly dynamic UAE property market. Through secure, professional services designed to optimize client investment returns, eqarat.com has seized the initiative in worldwide property e-solutions.

Looking at property thought different eyes - The mission

To take a holistic view of Real Estate, and then integrate their unique bouquet of solutions and services to realize this view – is the primary focus at eqarat.com. Their core-business supporting activities from Marketing, Sales, Customer Support, Leasing and Property Management to online services, are the arsenals in fulfilling the promise of being a turnkey Real Estate Property Solutions Provider.

Not just sight, but foresight – The vision

- Identify unique investment opportunities within the Real Estate sector for investors, customers, partners and service providers
- Revolutionize the way to conduct business in real estate through deploying state-of-the-art business modes, systems and processes
- Be the market leader in specialized property selling and buying
- Make available to clients up-to-date, genuine information and data relevant to the Real Estate Market
- Identify and procure the ideal property and investment for clients, in tune with their lifestyles
- Establish a Global Agents Network and provide a service centre for the agents where they can have access to all eqarat.com information through the portal
- Allow clients and agents around the globe to utilize the advanced portal platform, enabling them to conduct business in a more efficient and dynamic manner.

Since its genesis in 1991, eqarat.com has evolved and grown exponentially. They have now positioned themselves as one of the leading Real Estate Total Solutions Providers not only in the region but globally as well. They can now confidently and proudly claim to hold a unique and forefront position in the global market.

With new offices in Oman, Kuwait and Jordan, eqarat.com has continuing expansion plans throughout the region and globally. As a result of the phenomenal growth and the ever growing demands from Real Estate prospects, the company is intending in the near future to expand its operations to Saudi Arabia, Morocco, India and the UK.

eqarat.com also continually expands and invests in its human resources. Multi-cultured, well educated, and extremely knowledgeable - the staff have an edge when it comes to identifying the best investment opportunities in the region and dealing with elite customers. The company provides specialized and focused training to its team members in the areas of Property Consulting Services, Customer Relations, Market Updates and Research, etc.

Company Services

eqarat.com is continually researching and applying fresh methods. The company's goal is to provide their agents with the required tools they require to sell more property. They proactively increase and re-define the marketing strategy by combining run-of-the-mill marketing opportunities with other up-and-coming outlets to increase brand awareness and increase their market share each year.

The company provides a wide range of property services, from property consultancy to property sales services for both individual buyers and sellers. A professional dedicated team of real estate experts is continually soliciting high value projects for prospective investors and developers across the globe. The company's reach is limitless, and the overall objective is to satisfy client requirements and maximize their investment returns.

Property investment vehicles and core-business supporting activities including property management, entertainment, mortgages, online services, communication and IT support – are the arsenal in fulfilling the promise of being a turnkey Real Estate Property Solutions Provider. The company's umbrella of real state companies, architects, contractors, banks and real state owners are the vital cogs in taking the eqarat.com brand philosophy to a global plane.

The perfect business partner who will rightly identify your investment opportunity while simplifying the search process and dramatically expands your property investment choices. Whether you are a realtor, a personal investor or a developer, with EQARAT.COM – YOUR SEARCH ENDS HERE.

eqarat.com
P.O. Box 7553, Dubai
United Arab Emirates

Tel: +971 4 3242224
Fax: +971 4 3242221
Email: info@eqarat.com
Website: www.eqarat.com

3d- Venture Real Estate

Tel: +971 4 3593535

Fax: +971 4 3593536

Website: www.3d-venture.com

AAA Home/Web Real Estate

Tel: +971 4 3689999

Fax: +971 4 3626161

Website: www.dubaiaaa.com

aaproperty.ae

Tel: +971 6 800264

Fax: +971 6 7424000

Website: www.aaproperty.ae

Abraj Property Developers

Tel: +971 4 3377977

Fax: +971 4 3377855

Website: www.abrajdubai.com

Akar Properties

Tel: +971 4 3491999

Toll Free: 800 2527

Fax: +971 4 3499998

Website: www.akar.ae

Al Derea Real Estate Brokerage

Tel: +971 4 3214442

Fax: +971 4 3211443

Website: www.silicongatesdubai.com

Al Hathboor Real Estate

Tel: +971 4 2821124

Fax: +971 4 2821922

Website: www.alhathboor.com

Al Odaid Real Estate Co. LLC

Tel: +971 2 6262525

Toll free: 800 ODAID (800 63243)

Fax: +971 2 6277630

Website: www.alodaid.ae

Al Khayat Real Estate

Tel: +971 4 3978111

Fax: +971 4 3977322

Website: www.alkhayat.ae

Al Zad Real Estate

Tel: +971 4 3355714

Fax: +971 4 3355247

Website: www.alzadrealestate.com

Alich Real Estate Broker LLC

Tel: +971 4 2272858

Fax: +971 4 2272859

Website: www.alichrealestate.ae

Alpha Properties

Tel: +971 4 2288588

Fax: +971 4 2287080

Website: www.alphaproperties.com

Arabian Home Real Estate

Tel: +971 4 2953838

Fax: +971 4 2953737

Website: www.arabianhomes.org

Arenco Real Estate

Tel: +971 4 3572402

Fax: +971 4 3375335

Website: www.arencore.com

Ariha Commerical Broker LLC
Tel: +971 4 3960110
Fax: +971 4 3970110
Website: www.ariha-uae.ae

Aramada Group
Tel: +971 4 3317222
Fax: +971 4 3316565
Website: www.armadaholding.com

aryene. com
Tel: +971 4 3526367
Fax: +971 4 3526368
Website: www.aryene.com

Aspire Real Estate
Tel: +971 4 3390123
Fax: +971 4 3390164
Website: www.aspiredubai.com

Asteco Property Management
Tel: +971 4 4037700
Fax: +971 4 4037778
Website: www.asteco.com

Awazi Gargash Properties LLC
Tel: +971 4 2221277
Fax: +971 4 2227797
Website: www.gargashproperties.ae

Barclays Real Estate
Tel: +971 4 3593591
Fax: +971 4 3593592
Website: www.barclaysuae.com

Bavaria Gulf Real Estate
Tel: +971 4 3298880
Fax: +971 4 3298813
Website: www.bavariagulf.com

Belhasa International Company LLC
Tel: +971 4 2662319
Fax: +971 4 2623809
Website: www.belhasa.com

Better Homes
Tel: +971 4 3447714
Fax: +971 4 3494449
Website: www.bhomes.com

Best Homes Real Estate
Tel: +971 4 3311133
Fax: +971 4 3322336
Website: www.besthomesemirates.com

Bond Real Estate
Tel: +971 4 3689988
Fax: +971 4 3689977
Website: www.bondrealestate.com

Choice Real Estate Consultancy
Tel: +971 4 3316499
Fax: +971 4 3316704
Website: www.choicegroup.info

Century 21 Gulf Group Real Estate
Tel: +971 4 2668121
Fax: +971 4 2663621
Website: www.century21gulfgroup.com

Cluttons
Tel: +971 4 3348585
Fax: +971 4 3348362
Website: www.cluttons.com/dubai

Colliers International Property Consultants
Tel: +971 4 3358676
Fax: +971 4 3358674
Website: www.colliers.com

Continental Real Estate
Tel: +971 4 2225586
Fax: +971 4 2225582
Website: www.continentalrst.com

Conqueror Real Estate
Tel: +971 4 3419444
Fax: +971 4 3419449
Website: www.conquerordubai.com

Corner Stone Real Estate
Tel: +971 2 6657055
Fax: +971 2 6655672
Website: www.cornerstone-uae.com

Creative Concepts Real Estate LLC
Tel: +971 4 2229007
Fax: +971 4 2221130
Website: www.crecons.com

Dheeraj & East Coast LLC
Tel: +971 4 3417333
Fax: +971 4 3417373
Website: www.dheerajeastcoast.com

Desert Homes
Tel: +971 4 3210110
Fax: +971 4 3211136
Website: www.deserthome.ae

Desert Dream Real Estate
Tel: +971 4 3430305
Fax: +971 4 3434987
Website: www.dddubai.com

Diamond Home Properties
Tel: +971 4 3357600
Fax: +971 4 3357800
Website: www.diamondhomegroup.com

Donya Real Estate
Tel: +971 4 2292930
Fax: +971 4 2292950
Website: www.donyarealestate.net

Dubai Dunes
Tel: +971 4 3433315
Fax: +971 4 3433183
Website: www.dubaidunes.com

Dubai Investment Real Estate Co
Tel: +971 4 8852622
Fax: +971 4 8852520
Website: www.di-realestate.com

Dubai Premier Real Estate Broker LLC
Tel: +971 4 3626123
Fax: +971 4 3626321
Website: www.dubaipremier.com

Dubai Vacation Homes
Tel: +971 4 3626345
Fax: +971 4 3626321
Website: www.d-vh.com

Dubai Waterfront Properties
Tel: +971 4 3213344
Fax: +971 4 3433022
Website: www.dubaiwaterfront.com

Emirates House Real Estate
Tel: +971 4 3434014
Fax: +971 4 3435015
Website: www.emiratesestate.com

Engel & Völkers
Tel: +971 4 3388104
Fax: +971 4 3388105
Website: www.engelvoelkers.com

Escan Real Estate
Tel: +971 2 4474202
Fax: +971 2 4473808
Website: www.escan.ae

eqarat.com
Tel: +971 4 3242224
Fax: +971 4 3242221
Website: www.eqarat.com

Exquiste Homes
Tel: +971 4 3327353
Fax: +971 4 3327352
Website: www.exqhomes.com

Falak Properties
Tel: +971 4 3441100
Toll Free: 800 432 525
Fax: +971 4 3441110
Website: www.falakproperties.com

Fakhruddin Properties
Tel: +971 4 3218852
Fax: +971 4 3218853
Website: www.fakhruddin.com

Fortune Real Estate
Tel: +971 4 3354540
Fax: +971 4 3353140
Website: www.fortunesdubai.com

Greenshield
Tel: +971 4 3974981
Fax: +971 4 3974982
Website: www.greenshield.co.ae

Group Seven Properties LLC
Tel: +971 4 3663377
Fax: +971 4 3663360
Website: www.group7properties.com

Habiba Real Estate
Tel: +971 4 2240707
Fax: +971 4 2240708
Website: www.habibare.com

Halcon Real Estate
Tel: +971 4 3619040
Fax: +971 4 3619041
Website: www.halconrealestate.com

Homeland Properties LLC
Tel: +971 4 3930400
Fax: +971 4 3931466
Website: www.homeland-dubai.com

Kleindienst & Partner
Tel: +971 4 3369902
Fax: +971 4 3350960
Website: www.kleindienst.ae

Key 2 Dubai
Tel: +971 4 3211353
Fax: +971 4 3211352
Website: www.key2dubai.ae

Lakeside Realty
Tel: +971 4 3211944
Fax: +971 4 3211904
Website: www.lakeside-real-estate.com

Lake View Real Estate
Tel: +971 4 3978987
Fax: +971 4 3978979
Website: www.lakeviewuae.ae

Landmark Properties
Tel: +971 4 3316161
Fax: +971 4 3314949
Website: www.landmark-dubai.com

Liwa Property Management
Tel: +971 4 3362929
Fax: +971 4 3362933
Website: www.liwaproperty.com

Long Coast Real Estate
Tel: +971 2 6817779
Fax: +971 2 6811105
Email: info@longcoast-uae.com
Website: www.longcoast-uae.com

Luxury Homes LLC
Tel: +971 4 3039300
Fax: +971 4 3039301
Website: www.dubailuxuryhomes.com

Luxury Real Estate Development LLC
Tel: +971 2 6411833
Fax: +971 2 6421804
Website: www.luxurydevelopment.ae

Makaseb Holdings Ltd
Tel: +971 4 3298454
Fax: +971 4 3298455
Website: www.makasebltd.com

Majestic Homes Real Estate
Tel: +971 4 3290735
Fax: +971 4 3290855
Website: www.majestichomesdubai.com

Manazel Real Estate
Tel: +971 2 6326556
Fax: +971 2 6326557
Website: www.manazel-re.com

Madain Properties
Tel: +971 4 3388991
Fax: +971 4 3388944
Website: www.madain.ae

Milford Real Estate LLC
Tel: +971 4 3328811
Fax: +971 4 3312138

MKO Real Estate
Tel: +971 4 2833733
Fax: +971 4 2833788
Website: www.mkore.com

My Dream Property
Tel: +971 4 2663026
Fax: +971 4 2663027
Website: www.mydreamproperty.ae

New Market Real Estate
Tel: +971 4 2865557
Fax: +971 4 2862647
Website: www.newmarketdubai.com

Newworld Real Estate
Tel: +971 4 3619955
Fax: +971 4 3619944
Website: www.newworlddubai.com

Ocean Front Real Estate
Tel: +971 4 3433256
Fax: +971 4 3433260

Olympus Properties
Tel: +971 4 3216550
Fax: +971 4 3216551
Website: www.olympuspropertiesdubai.ae

Oryx Real Estate
Tel: +971 4 3515770
Fax: +971 4 3515772
Website: www.oryxrealestate.com

Paramount Properties
Tel: +971 4 3518830
Fax: +971 4 3518831
Website: www.paramount4me.com

Parkvale Real Estate
Tel: +971 4 3416800
Fax: +971 4 3416500
Website: www.parkvalegroup.com

Palma Real Estate
Tel: +971 4 3619333
Fax: +971 4 3615433
Website: www.palma-re.com

Pegasus Realty LLC
Tel: +971 4 3290022
Fax: +971 4 3311989
Website: www.pegasusgroup.com.tr

Plus Properties
Tel: +971 2 6223316
Fax: +971 2 6223317
Website: www.plusproperties.ae

Premier Real Estate Bureau LLC
Tel: +971 4 3487572
Fax: +971 4 3487573
Website: www.prebdubai.com

Priority Real Estate
Tel: +971 4 3434433
Toll Free: 800 PRIORITY (800 77467489)
Fax: +971 4 3439177
Website: www.prioritydubai.com

Profile Group Properties
Tel: +971 2 6450545
Fax: +971 2 6450543
Website: www.profilegroup.ae

Property Network
Tel: +971 4 3329733
Fax: +971 4 3329755
Website: www.propertynetwork.ae

propertyfinder.ae
Tel: +971 4 3432270
Fax: +971 4 3432280
Website: www.propertyfinder.ae

Prudential Properties
Tel: +971 4 3374434
Fax: +971 4 3360091
Website: www.prudentialicm.com

Reef Real Estate Investment Co. LLC
Tel: +971 4 3293330
Fax: +971 4 3293331
Website: www.reefrealestate.net

Richland
Tel: +971 4 3218777
Fax: +971 4 3218778
Website: www.richlanddubai.com

Rocky Real Estate
Tel: +971 4 3532000
Fax: +971 4 3533388
Website: www.rockyrealestate.com

Rufi Real Estate
Tel: +971 4 2247352
Fax: +971 4 2247362
Website: www.rufireal.com

Rustar Real Estate
Tel: +971 4 3323336
Fax: +971 4 3316222
Website: www.rustar.ae

Sama Emirates Real Estate
Tel: +971 4 3215252
Fax: +971 4 3215533
Website: www.samaemirates.net

Sherwoods Independent Property Consultants
Tel: +971 4 3438002
Fax: +971 4 3438004
Website: www.sherwoodsproperty.com

Sheffield Holding Ltd
Tel: +971 4 2831414
Fax: +971 4 2833144
Website: www.sre.ae

Smart Homes
Tel: +971 4 2699133
Fax: +971 4 2698982
Website: www.smarthomes.ae

Smart Moves Real Estate
Tel: +971 4 3212644
Fax: +971 4 3212944
Website: www.smartmoves-dubai.com

Sweet Homes Real Estate
Tel: +971 4 2955640
Fax: +971 4 2955641
Website: www.sweethomesuae.com

The Real Estate Specialists
Tel: +971 4 3312662
Fax: +971 4 3312004
Website: www.thespecialistsdubai.com

The One Real Estate
Tel: +971 4 2254800
Fax: +971 4 2295380
Website: www.theone-uae.com

Top Class Real Estate Brokers LLC
Tel: +971 4 4224633
Fax: +971 4 4224634
Website: www.topclassreslestate.com

Ultimate Real Estate
Tel: +971 4 3431070
Fax: +971 4 3430988
Website: www.ultimate-estate.com

Usos International LLC
Tel: +971 4 2087400
Fax: +971 4 2087433
Website: www.usos.ae

Vakson Real Estate
Tel: +971 4 3939977
Fax: +971 4 3937494
Website: www.vakson.com

Vista Real Estate LLC
Tel: +971 4 3499060
Fax: +971 4 3442426

Wentworth Real Estate
Tel: +971 4 3297776
Fax: +971 4 3297767
Website: www.wentworthgroup.ae

Zagy Property
Tel: +971 4 2289105
Fax: +971 4 2289106
Website: www.hemsonsgroup.com

Finance

EFG - Hermes

EFG-Hermes is the Arab world's premier investment banking firm and the market leader in securities brokerage, asset management, investment banking, private equity and research.

EFG-Hermes was established in 1984. In July 1998, EFG-Hermes went public with a USD 50 million GDR offering and now boasts a market capitalization in excess of USD 2.5 billion. EFG-Hermes is listed on the Cairo and Alexandria (CASE) and London stock exchanges.

In February 2006, EFG-Hermes UAE was also granted a license to conduct brokerage activities from within the DIFC and became a member of the Dubai International Financial Exchange (DIFX), its wholesale exchange. EFG-Hermes is the first regional financial institution to broker that market alongside Barclays Capital, Credit Suisse, Citigroup, Deutsche Bank, HSBC, Morgan Stanley and UBS. The firm expects the DIFX to enhance capital mobility in the region and attract new international capital, creating additional regional and international opportunities for the firm and its clients.

The firm represents a customer base of nearly 40,000 clients from the Middle East, Europe and the United States.

Hot Market Cools Down

• **Maturing Property Market**: Over the past nine months, the residential property market in Dubai has continued to mature, with the four strongest signs of change being: i) a lower rate of price appreciation, ii) improvements in the legal framework, iii) an increasing level of activity in the secondary property market, and iv) a reduction in the number of new project launches.

• **Slow Pace of Project Handovers Affects Supply Forecasts**: Due to the slower pace of completed project handovers being witnessed this year, with approximately only 11,000 units of the expected 57,000 units coming on stream year-to-date, supply continues to lag far behind demand. This supply lag has prompted us to revise our housing unit supply forecasts for the next three to four years, with estimates of 25,000 housing units for the whole of 2007, 64,000 in 2008, and 68,000 in 2009.

• **Strong Demand for Dubai Property**: Demand for housing continues to rise as the population grows, mostly due to immigration. We maintain our assumption that the population of Dubai will rise to almost 1.9 million by 2010, up from 1.4 million today, implying a CAGR of 7.9%. We have revised our demand forecasts, which now call for demand of 45,000 to 50,000 units per annum.

• **Prices Begin to Fall in 2009**: Assuming that supply in 2007 is constrained, with the peak year of supply will be in 2009, the downturn will occur later than we had originally assumed. Our current forecast is for a rise in average prices of 10-15% in 2007 and a rise of 5-10% in 2008. We expect prices to peak in 2H2008 as more supply hits the market. We expect prices to start declining in 2009, which is now assumed to be the peak supply year, with a cumulative decline of 15-20% by 2011.

• **Price Correction will Encourage Stronger Demand**: Whilst we believe that there will be excess supply in 2008, we see this being absorbed by the pent-up demand of earlier years (2005-2007). We believe that the extent of the price correction that we are forecasting in 2009 will depend primarily on: i) The pace at which new units are delivered, and ii) the price elasticity of demand. We believe that demand is price elastic, and that once prices begin to come down from their highs, this will increase demand.

• **Rental Rates Look Set to Decline**: The rate of increase of rents has begun to slow. We expect the decline in the pace of rental rate growth observed in the first eight months of this year to be sustained into early 2008, with rents starting to decline in 2008 as new housing comes onto the market.

Price Stability and Legal Improvements Underscore Increased Maturity of Residential Property Market

Freehold market update

Price Stability

Among the strongest evidence that the Dubai property market has matured is the slowdown in the rise of selling prices. An in-house index that we have created to track properties in key areas across Dubai indicates that, overall, prices have increased by 13.9% in the eight months to August 2007. The index for villas rose by 16.4%, while that for apartments by 12.8%. During 2007, apartments made up a majority of the supply handed over, with these being concentrated in luxury developments such as Burj Dubai, Palm Jumeirah and Dubai Marina. It is interesting to note that the handover of units in these developments has created strong momentum in asking prices over the past few months.

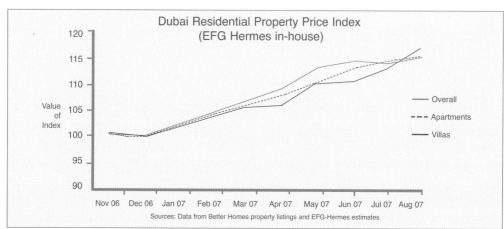

Dubai Residential Property Price Index (EFG Hermes in-house)

Sources: Data from Better Homes property listings and EFG-Hermes estimates

Legal Improvements

Over the past eight months, the introduction of new laws and increased legal clarity have provided support to the Dubai property market. These new elements include: i) the passing of the broker's law, ii) the establishment of the escrow law, iii) and the creation of the Real Estate Regulation Authority (RERA).

Effect of Handovers on The Property Market

Activity in the secondary market has been increasing as properties are handed over: i) Endusers are more comfortable buying a home they can actually see, and ii) many original owners, hoping for maximum returns, had been holding onto unfinished homes until they were close to completion or were completed. However, the fact that the pace of project handovers is not occurring at the expected pace is reducing available supply and thus continues to put upward pressure on prices.

Impact of New Project Launches

It is interesting to note that there have been relatively few new project launches over the past eight months, and those that have been launched have targeted specific markets. YTD, there have been around 35 new launches with four on average per month, which compares to more than 70 project launches in 2006 according to our estimates. The new launches are targeting mainly the mid-income or luxury segments. Some projects, such as golf course homes, have been oriented towards lifestyle communities. Recently, developers have also turned towards all-villa type projects in keeping with the high demand for spacious family homes.

Leasehold market update

Rent increases in the leasehold market have begun to soften. According to our estimates, the average YTD increase in residential rates in Dubai is 16% versus 30% in 2006, and 40% in 2005.

The government rent cap has limited increases, but because it does not apply to new contracts, some landlords continue to renew leases at higher than allowed levels. Dubai has set up a rent committee to deal with the problem, but not all cases get heard. Some landlords have also begun adding hefty maintenance charges to the annual rent that are in essence undeclared rent increases. We continue to divide the leasehold segment into: i) low-cost housing, ii) units targeting the middle-income segment, and iii) units targeting the high-end segment. According to our estimates, low and mid-income housing units have seen average rental increases of 14.2% and 15.3% respectively since the beginning of this year, down from 28.8% and 25.1% in 2006. The smaller rental increase seen in the mid-income housing segment in 2007 can be explained in part by people moving to less expensive areas further from the center of the city, such as International City, and in part by the fact that the rental increases of last year were from a relatively low base.

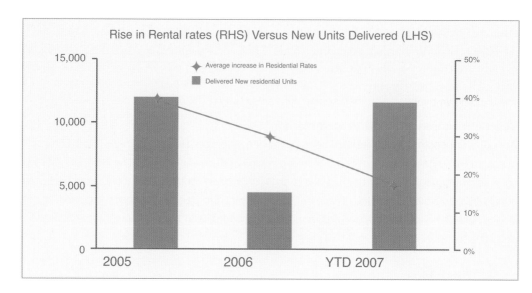

Slower Than Anticipated Delivery of Supply - We Revise our Supply Estimates

Another change this year is the slower pace of completed project handovers, a development that is delaying the surge in residential units supplied. Of our initial expectations of supply of 57,000 units (assuming project delays) to be handed over in 2007, we estimate that approximately 11,000 units have been handed over so far. By year end we expect no more than 25,000 units to have been delivered over the full year. These delays stem from: i) a lack of qualified contractors and labor, ii) increasing costs of construction and iii) an insufficient supply of construction machinery and equipment.

This slower pace of deliveries has prompted us to revise our expectations of the number of units that will come on stream over the next three to four years. We now believe that supply will be staggered, such that in any given year, 50-60% on average, of announced units will actually be handed over. In addition, we anticipate that the delivery of supply delayed in one year will cascade onto the two subsequent years. Thus, for 2008, we estimate 64,000 units will come on stream. This figure comprises of two-thirds of the supply we had originally estimated to be delivered in 2008, with the remainder representing the estimated spillover from 2007. We now expect the peak year of supply to be 2009, with 68,000 units being delivered. Like our new 2008 supply estimates, this is made up of the bulk of supply announced for 2009 being delivered as expected, in addition to the spillover from 2007 and 2008.

Our old no-delays scenario estimated 2008 supply at about 139,000 units - a scenario in which we had limited confidence in due to the fact that the bulk of supply to be handed over (80%) was being undertaken by private developers. Thus, we went on to assume that only 50% of planned 2008 supply (68,000 units) would actually be delivered. We further revise our expectations, adopting our new framework for estimating supply which accounts for delays and assumes supply spillovers into subsequent years. Our new estimate for 2008 supply is only slightly down from our previous estimate, at 64,000 housing units. This comprises of two-thirds of the supply we had originally estimated to be delivered in 2008, with the remainder representing the estimated spillover from 2007. The change in our estimates is illustrated in the figure below, with the breakdown between "original" supply and "spillover" supply illustrated.

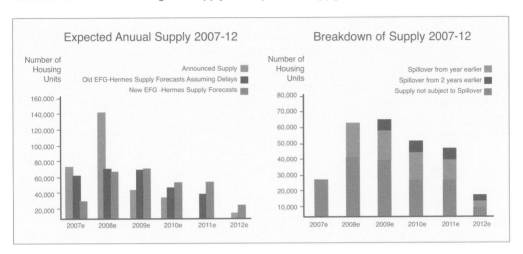

Strong Demand Continues - International Interest is Increasing

Demand for housing continues to rise as the population grows, mostly due to immigration. Robust economic fundamentals, high and rising oil prices and increasing wealth has washed the region with liquidity. Given the market's increasing sophistication and maturity, we have refined our assumptions, as we did with our supply estimates, and revised our forecasts for the demand for Dubai housing units. We maintain our assumption that the population of Dubai will rise to almost 1.9 million by 2010 from 1.4 million now, implying a CAGR of 7.9%. Using this as a base, we then segmented the market into local, expatriate and foreign demand and made assumptions about each group's propensity to buy homes in Dubai over the coming few years.

We arrive at an average demand of 45,000 to 50,000 units per annum. Local and expatriate demand, reinforced by a constant flow expatriates into the city and by existing residents seeking to buy their own residences, makes up the majority of our forecast demand. We also assume demand to be price elastic, such that demand will increase once prices fall from current levels due to increased supply.

Dubai continues to be a pioneer in terms of developing a liberal property market, with its initiatives towards improving the legal framework as well as market data increasing international interest. Real estate agents have also suggested that this revived interest has been helped by the handover of properties such as Palm Jumeirah, JBR and other Emaar projects (i.e. units in the Downtown Burj). The fact that Dubai real estate prices are on average competitive compared to those in major developed cities has helped spur demand.

Because of a lack of documented data on the breadth of international demand, we have estimated foreign interest based largely on anecdotal evidence. Buyer interest has largely been concentrated towards luxury or holiday homes, but more recently it seems that international investors are looking at certain types of Dubai property as good investment properties as well.

We believe that there still exists a layer of speculative demand. While speculation has decreased as the pace of price appreciation has slowed, it is still substantial, helped by the delay in supply, and the implicit leverage built into off-plan payment programs.

As described earlier, we believe demand to be price elastic. Should prices fall in 2009, when we expect supply to peak, we believe there will be a resulting increase in demand - especially stemming from mid-income expatriates - looking for homes to buy and live in.

Freehold Residential Outlook

We now expect the year of price correction to be 2009 rather than 2008. Whilst we believe that there will be excess supply in 2008, we see this being absorbed by the pent-up demand of earlier years (2005-2007). We forecast a rise in average prices of 10-15% in 2007 and a rise of 5-10% in 2008, with the peak being reached in 2H2008. Finally, we expect prices to start declining in 2009, with a cumulative decline of 15-20% by 2011.

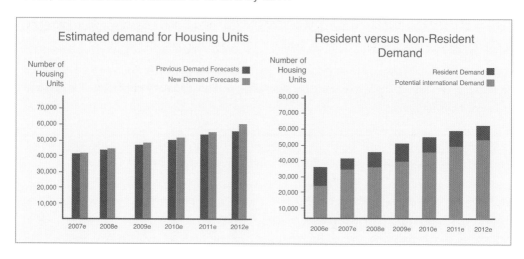

However, it is crucial to note that our assumptions and estimates entail a strong degree of subjectivity and potentially produce a wide range of potential price decline outcomes. The most important factor to bear in mind is that the extent of the correction will vary depending on whether the project lies in the low, mid or high segment.

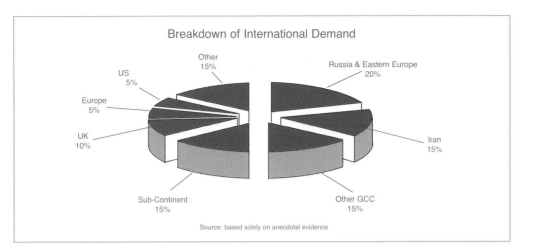

Breakdown of International Demand

Other 15%

Russia & Eastern Europe 20%

US 5%

Europe 5%

UK 10%

Iran 15%

Sub-Continent 15%

Other GCC 15%

Source: based solely on anecdotal evidence

Residential Rental Market Outlook

On average, Dubai residential rents across Dubai increased by 16% in the first eight months of 2007 versus 30% for the whole of 2006. We believe this trend of slowing rental rate increases stems from i) delays in expected supply coming on stream, ii) relief from the 7% rent cap for 2007 which has capped expectations, and iii) end-user demand for mid-income housing being higher than that for luxury housing, which has dominated delivered supply to date. Our expectation is that the rent cap for 2008 will most likely be reduced to 5%. Therefore, we expect the decline in the pace of rental rate growth observed in the first eight months of this year to continue into early 2008, with rents starting to decline in 2008 as new housing comes onto the market.

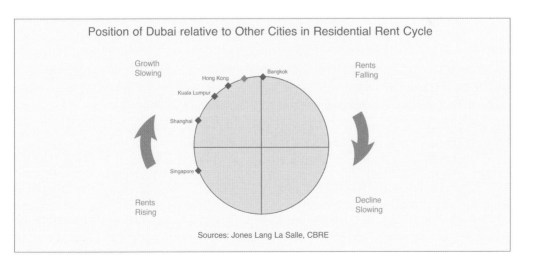

Position of Dubai relative to Other Cities in Residential Rent Cycle

Growth Slowing

Hong Kong

Bangkok

Rents Falling

Kuala Lumpur

Shanghai

Singapore

Rents Rising

Decline Slowing

Sources: Jones Lang La Salle, CBRE

Commercial Property Segment -
Rents and Prices Continue to Rise due to Capacity Limitations

As Dubai continues to attract businesses from across the globe, we have seen continued pressure in terms of both rents and selling prices of commercial property over the past 8 months.

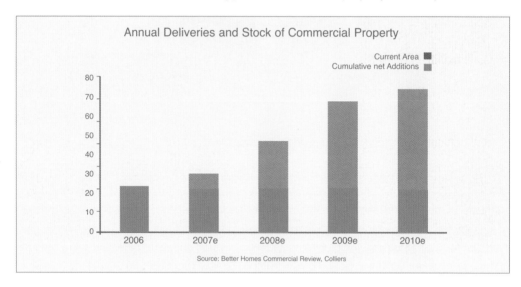

Vacancy rates of around 1%, in addition to pent-up demand from existing businesses and new tenants wishing to upgrade office premises has allowed rents to rise 40% YTD on average. Prices for freehold office space have risen 17% YTD. This trend of a sustained increase both in terms of rents and selling prices stems from a prolonged lag in the completion of new commercial supply. Most of the commercial space additions are expected to hit the market in 2008 and 2009 and we expect to see a marked decline in rents. As a result, we expect to see Dubai commercial property yields sliding back gradually toward the international average.

Sana Kapadia - Research Analyst
EFG-Hermes Dubai
Level 6, The Gate, West Wing, DIFC, Dubai
United Arab Emirates

Tel: +971 4 3634000
Fax: +971 4 3621170
Website: www.efg-hermes.com

The author has been in Dubai for 10 years and **Globaleye** have been exceeding the needs of investors in the region with an enviable position as the leader in financial services for the Middle East. With over 3500 clients, Globaleye are also recognized as the leading provider for property related services.

Before you buy

Buying a house is probably the largest investment most people will make. Whether it's a cottage in the country, a penthouse in the city or a villa on the Costa – in order to make your property dreams come to life you need to have your finances in order. Property mania has certainly hit Dubai and there are numerous high quality projects available from studio apartments to lavish townhouses. With new developments launched almost every week, the healthy Dubai property market has become the focus for investors from around the world. If you are considering buying property whether in Dubai or abroad, there are number of factors which you should consider. Here are just some questions that should feature high on your list…

What mortgage facilities are available?

There are literally thousands of mortgage options when buying in Europe or the UK. In the United Arab Emirates, however, the choice of Lenders is not as widespread and the options not as attractive as those found internationally. At present, typically you can borrow at ~8.25% in Dirhams for the various property developments that are regularly advertised in the local Press. Unfortunately, banks based overseas cannot provide lending facilities on UAE properties directly so one is confined to the locally established Lenders. Not all Lenders offer facilities on all the projects in Dubai – probably only half of the projects are financeable. It is important to obtain written confirmation from your Realtor/Developer that finance is available. This situation should change with the development of the Dubai Property Law which is great news for consumers. Hopefully more Lenders will enter the market, make borrowing more competitive and offer more solutions for various developments.

The typical mortgage in Dubai is on a Capital Repayment basis and you can obtain lending as high as 95% Loan-to-Value (LTV). For non-residents lending is often capped at 75% LTV so bear this in mind before you put your deposit down. Lenders in Dubai operate on an affordability calculation ensuring that your mortgage payment is not more than 50% of your monthly income, which includes other credit liabilities such as loans or other mortgages.

Typical documentation required will be ID, proof of residency, 6-month bank statements and a salary certificate if employed. If you are self-employed, you can expect the above plus 2 years audited accounts and 18 months business bank statements. Currently there is no form of adverse credit or self-certification mortgages so remember not to assume the finance will be available just because you can borrow in your home country.

That said, finance can be arranged through overseas Lenders if you have assets overseas too. A number of property investors with assets overseas have taken advantage of favourable international interest rates. For example, someone with property in the UK may be able to release equity to a maximum of 80% of the value of their property (less any outstanding mortgage) to finance all or part of their property purchase in Dubai. Interest rates can be secured as low as ~5% in £ terms as opposed to 8.25% in Dirhams locally.

One should be aware of the additional costs for arranging finance – your bank may levy a fee and once again international Lenders tend to offer very competitive terms. Valuation fees, Brokers Costs, Protection fees, legal/conveyancing and in some cases planning permission can all add to the costs.

If you do not have overseas property to obtain finance then another form of collateral could be an investment portfolio which could be used as security to obtain a loan. Once again, depending on the assets within the portfolio, a bank would be willing to offer a loan using the portfolio as security. This alleviates having to liquidate assets in a portfolio which in turn could be making sufficient returns to meet the interest payments. Obviously one should be aware of the currency differential but on the whole the savings in interest are so great that the option of overseas mortgages are really worth considering.

It is worth exploring all the options and seek independent advice. Since there are so many international mortgage solutions available, get the one that is right for you. If you do not have assets elsewhere then your options are limited to those offered by the lending terms of the local banks of the UAE.

Do I need to get insurance?

Most Lenders (i.e. banks and building societies) will require some form of protection for the loan. This makes a lot of sense since you want your property to be paid off in the event of your death or diagnosis of a serious/terminal illness. Banks on the whole do not like repossessing property and would prefer the loan to be repaid from an insurance policy should a serious event occur. Similarly, if you had to sell the property to pay the loan in the absence of a policy, the value of the property may have fallen to a level below the outstanding loan amount. Moreover, if the reason you cannot pay your mortgage is because you are terminally ill, you certainly do not want to be homeless as well. With critical illness affecting 1 in 4 of us at some stage in our life, many Lenders will require that you have sufficient protection to cover the amount of loan you have secured.

Seeking the right insurance is key since it comes in many forms. Whole of Life, Term, Endowment are all widely available in the UAE – get the right advice to determine which one is right for you. Similarly, it pays to use a Broker since they can normally secure terms well below that which is offered directly by most Lenders. Be aware of Affinity Schemes that are offered by

Banks typically since they are more expensive than securing your own insurance.

Remember, if your loved one passes away, unfortunately the bills do not go with them – avoid the financial trauma and have yourself correctly protected.

Which property should I go for?

We do not select or recommend property developments to our customers – we just arrange the financial aspects of the deal. It pays to select an agent once again who can run you through all the developments available so the right solution is selected. Pick someone who has a good experience of the local market and is not constrained to one or two developments. Local knowledge is key and a good agent should be able to guide you through the whole process of your purchase.

How do I go about buying?

Once you have set your heart on the property you require there are going to be a number of issues that need addressing. Here are just a few to run through ...

1. Can you afford it? More importantly are you prepared for the property to go down in value as well as up? Property is just like any other investment and can fluctuate according to the overall market. How long you are going to hold the property will determine whether you can be sure it will make money or not.

2. Can you afford it if the interest payments change? Lenders can alter the interest rate or the term potentially and this could have an impact on your monthly payments. Although interest rates are relatively low internationally, be prepared that they can rise. Check if you can pay off the loan early and if so are there any penalties in doing so? Can you change Lenders at a later stage?

3. Consider the potential currency fluctuation. Whatever your reasons for buying foreign currency, when buying a property abroad you will certainly be looking to benefit from the best possible exchange rates. A favourable rate can mean the difference of hundreds, if not thousands, of $/£/€ on a large-scale transaction. Working with a wholesale currency trader can advise you whether to move your money now, later or phase payment and reduce your fees for TT with the better rates than your Bank most of the time.

4. Can you afford the transaction costs? Typically local lenders are charging 1% of the loan value as a processing fee not to mention the insurance element too. Have you budgeted for legal, protection and any other conveyancing type costs? Transfer fees 1.5%, real estate agent fees 2%.

5. What are the ongoing maintenance costs of your property and the communal areas and are they due to rise – if so by what amount? Who controls the rise in maintenance fees – developer or the residents? Is there any form of Residents Committee?

6. Do you need to purchase through an Offshore Company or Trust? Property Law in Dubai is based under Sharia principles and as such in the event of the demise of your husband for example the property may bypass the wife as the new legal owner. Can you sell the property

on without restrictions? Similarly, you may wish to mitigate your death tax exposure by using some form of offshore structure. Buying property in Dubai will not avoid death taxes from your home country unless structured correctly.

7. Since you are indeed expanding your asset base it is wise to review your Will. Unless you make a Will, you cannot guarantee that your belongings, when you die, will be distributed as you wish. Many unnecessary complications arise, adding to the grief of the bereaved and the expense of winding up the estate. If you die without a Will (`intestate`) the law decides who will receive your possessions. In addition to your Will you should also consider an Enduring Power of Attorney (EPA). This document will allow your designated executors to manage your affairs in the event of you becoming incapacitated either mentally or through injury. Remember, the Will only takes effect in the event of your demise so to avoid excessive dealings with the Public Guardianship office, an EPA will give clear instructions and allow your affairs to be managed.

8. Have you sought professional help with protecting the property should a serious event occur? Life Cover, Income Protection, Critical Illness Cover, Permanent & Total Disability in their various forms should be reviewed and budgeted for.

9. Have you made provision for Home & Contents cover to meet the eventualities of owning property? Ensure you have selected a large insurer who will be on hand to settle claims quick and efficiently.

Do I need an offshore Company?

There are numerous reasons but with regards to property it achieves 3 main objectives if established correctly.

- You may wish to buy in the name of the Offshore Company in order to conceal the name of the beneficial owners. This is particularly useful when estate planning for investors who have death tax issues to mitigate. Of those Governments that impose death taxes, (e.g. Inheritance Tax in the UK) you will be taxed on your worldwide estate in the event of death. "Worldwide estate" is the key word since it is not just the assets you have at home. So for example, if you are a British domiciled person with houses in the UK, Dubai and Monte Carlo, on death you will be taxed at 40% on all assets including property after an allowance of £275,000. The 40% charge has been muted to rise to 50% very soon. Since the average cost of a house in the UK now is about £250,000 then there is a fairly big tax bill coming for your beneficiaries. The other key word is "domicile" - it does not matter how long you have lived overseas, if you were born or have spent a substantial period in the UK (more than 17years) you are deemed domicile. Trying to lose your domicile status is very difficult indeed. So, if an offshore company was established perhaps with the correct use of Nominee Directors and Trustees, this potentially huge tax bill can be mitigated.

- When buying in Dubai for example, very few investors appreciate that the legal system here is different to that they may have at home. In the event of death, the property does not necessarily pass to the wife since Sharia Law (the governing Islamic law of the UAE) determines otherwise as laid down in the Koran (An-Nisa Chapter 4 para 7 onwards). In order to ensure the property is passed on to those you wish, an offshore company could be established with the spouses as Directors. In the event of their demise the shares of company are passed on to the surviving spouse and beneficiaries. Although the spouse has died, the offshore company has not; thereby an internal transfer of shares circumvents this potential Sharia issue. Few investors in Dubai realty realise this potential problem and this also true for Emirati Nationals who buy in the UK. On their demise they would be liable for 40% death tax on assets they hold in the UK.

- Once again in Dubai, many speculative investors who purchase property with a view to re-selling after a profit is secured have to overcome the issues of transfer costs. Previously referred to as stamp duty in the UK, associated transfer costs when obtaining new ownership of property can be quite high and thereby eat into your re-sell profits. Dubai has transfer fees ranging from 1-4% depending on which project you are buying/selling. However, if the property was bought in the name of the offshore company then the transaction of ownership can be achieved by selling the offshore company. In essence, you sell your offshore company that owns a property and not the property itself. An offshore company should be used for each property you purchase to manage a portfolio effectively.

It should be noted that one has to decide which benefits are more crucial; the uses of an offshore company or obtaining finance for your property. At present, Dubai lenders are not offering loans to offshore companies so one needs to decide the priority.

Since buying a house is generally the largest investment most of us will ever do, it makes sense to explore all your options so you can be sure that what you are about to do will meet your needs now and for the foreseeable future. Seek the professional services of a good agent who is willing to spend time understanding your profile so the right properties are selected for you. Likewise, take guidance from a Lawyer if buying locally and employ a suitable conveyancing group when buying overseas. And finally, secure sound financial advice from an independent source so the various aspects (pitfalls) to property finance, insurance and offshore structures are discussed in full.

Happy house hunting!

Tim Searle
Globaleye Group
Villa #6, Jumeirah Beach Road,
P.O. Box 24592, Dubai, United Arab Emirates
Toll Free: 8004558
Tel: +9714 3489330
Fax: +9714 3489331
Website: www.globaleyegroup.com

Founded in 1690 by John Freame and Thomas Gould to serve the banking needs of the city of London, **Barclays Bank PLC** is today a global Financial Services provider engaged in Retail and Commercial Banking, Investment Banking, Wealth Management and Investment Management Services. Barclays Bank PLC is one of the largest financial services company in the world by market capitalisation, listed on the New York, London and Tokyo stock exchanges.

By putting customers at the heart of everything they do, executing flawlessly, innovating for success and developing their people, Barclays Bank aim to secure a position as the best retail and commercial bank, every market, every time.

Mortgages

Mortgages are offered to resident and non resident buyers of property in UAE and are available for owner occupied and buy-to-let properties. Barclays offers a comprehensive suite of mortgage products and is the first bank in the UAE to offer mortgages in foreign currencies including Pound Sterling, US Dollars and Euros along with loan up to an age of 70 years.

The team at Barclays constantly strives to improve the existing product offering and aligning it to the needs of both local and international buyers – to this effect the cue is taken from within the global Barclays network thereby maintaining its product pioneering traditions.

A vibrant and visible feature of Barclays Mortgages, that has fast become the talk of the town, are the Barclays Mini Coopers zipping around the roads of Dubai thereby allowing our mobile mortgage advisers to offer their expert advice to clients at their convenience.

At a glance, prominent features of Barclays Mortgages include:

1. Competitive Interest Rates – (BMR - Barclays Mortgage Rates)
2. Simple application process
3. Maximum loan up to 90% of the assessed value of the property (valuer's assessment) for villas developed by Master Developers
4. Expert Mobile Mortgage Advisors
5. Range of currencies available (AED, USD, GBP, EURO)
6. Max loan of up to AED 10 million
7. Residential and Buy-to-let mortgages available
8. Pay Interest only option also offered
9. Simple documentation requirements
10. Fast approvals
11. Mortgage offered for completed and off plan properties

Costs to Consider

As with buying a property anywhere in the world, there are a few costs to bear in mind when you purchase property in Dubai. These costs may consist of the following:

Arrangement or Loan Processing Fee
A fee of 1%-1.25% of the loan amount is charged as an arrangement fee by most lenders. Barclays Charges 1% of loan value for AED loans and 0.8% of loan value for currency loans.

Agents Fee
Estate agents or real estate agents charge 1%-2% of your property value as a fee.

Broker Fees
Property and mortgage arranged through a broker, would attract an additional charge around 1-2% of the property value.

Registration Fee
Dubai Lands Department would charge a fee of 1%-1.5% to register a property depending on the property type (villa or an apartment).

Mortgage Registration Fee at Lands Department
A fee of 0.25% on the loan is charged by Dubai Lands Department to register the mortgage.

Property Transfer Fee
A Property brought from the open market would attract a charge of 1% - 1.5% by the developer as transfer charges.

Mortgage Registration Fee

Since Title registration at Lands Department is undertaken in a phased manner, developers maintain an internal register and they register a mortgage in their internal registry for which a charge of AED 3,000- AED 5,000 is charged depending upon the developer.

Valuation Fee

A Flat fee of AED 3,000 is charged by most of the valuation companies and valuation of the property is insisted by most lenders.

Residential units from major developers like Emaar, Nakheel, Dubai Properties, ETA Star etc. are approved by Barclays

To find more on the Mortgage offering and any other fees and charges that may apply please call on 800 BARCLAYS (800 – 22725297) or mail at mortgages.uae@barclays.com alternatively you may log in to www.barclays.ae

Dubai Islamic Bank is the world's first Islamic Bank. It is a global leader and a pioneer in the Islamic Banking industry.

Over 30 years in Islamic Banking has given the bank the experience that allows them to offer comprehensive Islamic solutions for all your financial needs. They deliver this experience through the latest banking methods, state-of-the-art technology and commitment to flexibility and innovation.

At Dubai Islamic Bank Al Islami Home Finance offers you a range of finance solutions to suit your needs.

The Mobile Mortgage Service Advisors visit you at your convenience and take you through each step towards opening the door of your investment or home.

A unique range of products to choose from.

Forward Ijarah (Forward Lease) – Under Construction Property

This is a forward dated Ijara (lease) agreement with the Bank for a property to be delivered at a future date. This product is offered to customers interested in a property under construction. Dubai Islamic Bank will take over the developer's payment schedule and all payments will be made directly to the developer over the construction period.

Once the construction is complete the product work exactly like an Ijarah product. The payment to Bank starts after the property is handed over to the customer.

- Finance available up to 90% of property value
- Finance value up to AED 5 millions
- Flexible tenure up to 25 years
- Salary transfer not required
- Installments start only after the completion of the property
- Islamic insurance available
- Competitive profits rates

Ijarah (Standard)

This is a lease contract wherein the Bank (Lessor) leases the property to the customer (lessee) in return for a rental payment for a specified financing period. The Bank promises to transfer the title of the property to the customer at the end of the financing period if all payments have been made.

This product is offered to customers acquiring ready property. The customer has the option of the option of choosing from a variety of down payment, tenure and profit rate options. This is ideal for customers looking for an easy installment scheme.

Ijarah offers you installments at a variable profit rate, at the end of which you can own your home.

- Finance available up to 90% f property value
- Finance value up to AED 5 millions
- Flexible tenure up to 25 years
- Salary transfer not required
- Islamic insurance available
- Competitive profit rates

Commercial Finance

Dubai Islamic Bank provides finance to individuals either under Forward Ijarah for commercial properties such as office space, retail space, etc. This enables you to put your capital to other profitable uses and manage your cash flows better, especially when you are planning to start a business venture.

- Finance value up to AED 5 million
- Flexible tenure up to 15 years
- Salary transfer not required
- Islamic Insurance available
- Competitive profit rates

Advance Eligibility Process

Our unique Advance Eligibility Process service designed specially for UAE residents who have not yet selected their property and are unaware of their financial eligibility. It gives you the advantages of starting your search for a property with a confirmed and approved for finance based on your income and liabilities.

- Finance up to AED 5 million
- Tenure up to 25 years
- Conversion to mortgages-specific finance facilities
- Clarity about what you can afford
- Easy and simple documentation

Eligibility
Salaried:
- Minimum age 21 years – maximum age 60/70 years (Expatriate/UAE National)

- Salary AED 8000/AED 10,000 (UAE National/Expatriate)
- Finance amount AED 100,000 minimum and AED 5,000,000 maximum
- Finance to value 90% (unless otherwise specified)

Self-Employed

- Minimum age 21 years – maximum age 60/70 years (Expatriate/UAE National)
- Minimum 2 years length of business
- Finance amount AED 100,000 minimum and 5,000,000 maximum
- Finance to value 80% (unless otherwise specified)

Documentation

- 6 months' bank statement
- Salary letter (in case of non-salary transfer customer)
- Valid passport/Khulasat al Khaid copy
- Valid visa
- Relevant property papers
- Evaluation from approved evaluators
- Copy of trade license (Self-employed)
- Audited financial statements (Self-employed)
- Notarised POA (Where applicable for Self-employed)
- Memorandum and Articles of Association (Self-employed)

For more information, please visit any of the following Dubai Islamic Bank branches:

Al Shoala Branch

Umm Suqeim Branch

Al Barsha Branch

Dubai Internet City Branch

Abu Dhabi (Main Branch)

Sharjah (Main Branch)

For a visit from the Mobile Mortgage Sales Advisors,
Call 800 4766

In the coming years the number of banks set to offer mortgages is expected to rise. this information has been compiled from the websites of the respective financial institutions. The information was correct at the time of research of the subject.

Lender	Abu Dhabi Commercial Bank
Eligibility	UAE nationals, expatriates.
Mortgage term	25 years
Interest rate	Base rate plus 2.5% for the first year. Varying rate capped at 9.00% for three years. Varying rate capped at 9.50% for 5 years. Fixed rate of 8.50% for three years. Fixed rate of 9.00% for five years.
Maximum loan amount	As much as 90% finance offered, up to AED 3.5 million.
Insurance requirements	Life insurance, Loan insurance.
Minimum salary (AED)	10,000
Fees	Processing fee of 1%, minimum of AED 5,000.
Repayment penalty	3% of the outstanding, 5% if bank buyout.
Valuation fee	up to AED 3,000.
Eligible properties	Nakheel, Damac, Rose Tower 1, Sharjah. Emaar, Union Properties, Dubai Properties, Asteco, Al Dar, Areef.
Documentation	Passport copy, salary certificate, six months salary bank account statements, application form.

Lender	Lloyds TSB
Eligibility	UAE residents, non resident UK expatriates only
Mortgage term	15 years
Interest rate	7.5% variable, straight repayment mortgage. Lump sum repayments possible at no charge. Special rate of 6% offered for phase 2 of Greens Community.
Maximum loan amount	Depends on salary
Insurance requirements	Life cover is mandatory
Minimum salary (AED)	12,000
Fees	0.5% arrangement fee on completed application.
Valuation fee	of AED 2,500. Fees can be added to loan amount.
Repayment penalties	None
Eligible properties	Emaar, Jumeirah Beach Residence, UP (The Green Community and UPTOWN Mirdiff) and Nakheel
Documentation	Salary certificate, passport copies, six months bank statements agreement of property sale

Lender	Amlak (Shariah compliant)
Eligibility	UAE nationals, GCC residents, UAE residents and non-residents.
Mortgage term	Up to 15 years for GCC, UAE residents and non-residents, 25 years for UAE nationals from August 2005. Amlak offers all new UAE resident customers up to 20 years on villas and townhouses.
Interest rate	Variable rate (residents): 6.75% for 70% and below 6.95% for 80% finance, 7.25% for 90%, (non-residents 7.50%)
Fixed rate	(Residents): 7-15 yrs 10.50%; 5 - 7yrs. 8.75% Up to 5 yrs 8.00% (non-residents add 0.50%).
Maximum loan amount	Depends on salary.
Insurance requirements	Not compulsory. Islamic insurance solutions available. Property insurance is compulsory, family protection is not.
Minimum salary (AED)	N/A
Fees	No early settlement charge. No partial repayment charges, 1% processing fee - Min. AED 5,000, Non-residents-1.25% Min. - AED 5,000,
Valuation fee	Up to AED 3,000.
Eligible properties	Emaar, JBR, Al Fattan, Nakheel, Palm Developments.
Documentation	Passport, labour card, ID card, salary certificate, 6 months' bank statements, other income documents, copy of sale/purchase agreement, proof of downpayment, cheque for loan processing fee.

Lender	Habib Bank AG Zurich
Eligibility	UAE nationals and UAE residents.
Mortgage term	Up to 15 years.
Interest rate	3.5% above 1 year LIBOR, min. of 6.5% per annum.
Maximum loan amount	70% of loan to value ratio, up to AED 3,500,000.
Insurance requirements	Property and Life Insurance policies.
Minimum salary (AED)	12,000
Fees	1% of outstanding loan as early settlement charge. Processing fee1% of the loan amount, or min. AED 5,000.
Eligible properties	Emaar, Nakheel and Dubai Properties.
Documentation	For employed applicants - a salary transfer letter from the employer, (For business owners/directors - Trade Licence and audited company financials, passport copy, 6 months bank statement, property and life insurance policies.

Lender	HSBC Bank Middle East Limited
Eligibility	UAE and non-UAE residents.
Mortgage term	Up to 20 yrs. subject to repayment by 60th birthday. 20 yrs for villas and townhouse, 15 yrs for apartments.
Interest rate	Up to 70% = 6.75% variable, 70-80% = 7% variable. HSBC can help with stage payments required by approved developers using a Construction Finance Account, charged at 1.25% above the mortgage rate. Less 0.15% if salary transferred. Special rates offered for Phase 2 of Greens Community.
Maximum loan amount	Depends on individual financial status. Standard pre-completed properties-80% of developer price; completed properties-80% of market value as determined by an appointed valuer (valuation will be charged).
Insurance requirements	Mortgage protection policy and Buildings Insurance.
Minimum salary (AED)	Depends on financial status.
Fees	Can be viewed on www.uae.hsbc.com. 1% of the loan amount is levied as arrangement fee for the mortgage.
Eligible properties	Al Hamra Village in RAK, Marina Heights Tower, JBR, Al Nakheel,Greens Community, Emaar Villas & Townhouses (but not apartments).
Documentation	Passport, current salary certificate, six month's bank statements, credit card statement, other income documents, copy of sale/purchase agreement.

Lender	Mashreqbank
Eligibility	UAE residents and non–residents
Mortgage term	Up to 15 years
Interest rate	6.95% fixed till Dec. 2005, then 4.99% + 3 months EIBOR with a minimum of 6.95% for residents & non - residents. Varies depending on the property
Maximum loan amount	Up to 80% (of original property price) or max of AED 3 million
Insurance requirements	Life and Property Insurance mandatory
Minimum salary (AED)	10,000
Fees	1.23% processing fee on the loan amount
Eligible properties	Emaar Properties, Dubai Properties, Nakheel
Documentation	Application form, passport copy, bank statement, property documents etc.

Lender	National Bank of Abu Dhabi
Eligibility	UAE nationals, expatriates only in Abu Dhabi/Dubai
Mortgage term	Up to 25 years for all
Interest rate	Base rate + 1%.
Maximum loan amount	Up to AED 5 million.
Insurance requirements	Property and Life Insurance.
Minimum salary (AED)	10,000
Fees	Processing fee AED 1,500 Minimum of AED 5,000, repayment penalty of 1% of outstanding, or AED 10,000 whichever is greater.
Eligible properties	Residential only for expatriates.
Documentation	Passport copy, sale receipt, transfer documents, salary certificate, six months bank statements, application form.

Lender	National Bank of Dubai
Eligibility	UAE nationals, GCC residents, UAE residents and non-residents.
Mortgage term	20 yrs for UAE nationals, 15 yrs for expats, 12 yrs. for non residents.
Interest rate	7.65% on reducing balance basis. Special rates for Dubai
Properties	Business Bay.
Maximum loan amount	Multiples of salary for 60 months, or 80% of the property valuation (by the Land Department), whichever is lower.
Insurance requirements	Life and Property Insurance mandatory. Monthly premium. 0.40% per annum of the loan amount.
Minimum salary	(AED) 8,000 UAE nationals, 10,000 expatriates, 25,000 non-residents.
Fees	1% processing fee, or AED 5,000 whichever is higher.
Eligible properties	Emaar, Nakheel, JBR and Dubai Properties.
Documentation	Passport, labour card, ID card, salary certificate, six month's bank statements, other income docs, copy of sale/ purchase agreement, proof of downpayments, cheque for loan processing fee.

Lender	Tamweel (Shariah compliant)
Eligibility	UAE and non-UAE residents.
Mortgage term	5-25 years.
Interest rate	(Depends on scheme.) Floating Rate, which applies to loan tenors of 3-25 yrs. 7.25% (changes every six months). Fixed Rates, from- 8.95% depends on loan tenor. 'Yusr' Adjustable
Repayment offers	between 4.99% for 1 yr, 5.99% for 3 yrs.
Maximum loan amount	AED 5 million. Depends on salary and tenor.
Insurance requirements	Life insurance mandatory. Life/ Property if through Aman Insurance can be consolidated with the mortgage.
Minimum salary (AED)	Salaried 10,000, Self-employed 15,000.
Fees	Processing fee of 1.25%-minimum of AED 3,500 up to a maximum of AED 15,000. No early redemption fee. Service charge may be applicable.
Eligible properties	JBR, Nakheel, IFA, Aber, Deyaar, Emaar, Bonyan, Best Homes, Jade, Tulip, Sports City, 7 Tides, Asam, GGIC, Sondos.
Documentation	Application form, passport copy, labour Card, ID card, salary certificate, six months bank statements, copy of developer sale/ purchase agreement, downpayment receipt, cheque for loan processing fee.

Lender	Union National Bank (Dream Home Loan)
Eligibility	UAE nationals, expatriates.
Mortgage term	UAE nationals - 25 years. Expatriates - 20 years.
Interest rate	6.75% on a reducing balance basis Depends on downpayment 10% - 6.75% flat rate, 20% - 6.5%, 30% - 6.25% Plus average of ADIBOR and DIBOR.
Maximum loan amount	Up to AED 5 million.
Insurance requirements	Property and life insurance included in loan 0.45% of loan amount applied for 50% of loan tenor, paid in advance.
Minimum salary	(AED) 8,000
Fees	Processing fee or 1%, minimum of AED 5,000 Early repayment penalty of 1% of outstanding, 1.5% for a bank buyout.
Eligible properties	Emaar, Nakheel, JBR and Damac.
Documentation	Passport copy, employment letter covering salary certificate and length of service, salary transfer letter, six months bank statements, sale receipt, downpayment receipt, transfer documents, application form.

Lender	Barclays Bank
Eligibility	UAE and non-UAE residents.
Mortgage term	5-25 years.
Interest rate	7.75%-9.01%
Maximum loan amount	90% on the value of property for villas developed by Master Developers
Insurance requirements	Not Available
Minimum salary (AED)	Not Available
Fees	1% of loan amount
Eligible properties	Selected completed and off-plan properties
Documentation	Application form, passport copy, labour Card, ID card, salary certificate, six months bank statements, copy of developer sale/purchase agreement, downpayment receipt, cheque for loan processing fee.

Lender	Dubai Bank
Eligibility	UAE and non-UAE residents.
Mortgage term	Up to 20 years
Interest rate	Variable
Maximum loan amount	Up to 90% of property value
Insurance requirements	TBC
Minimum salary	(AED) 8,000
Fees	TBC
Eligible properties	All major developers, off-plan properties and secondary market properties
Documentation	Application form, passport copy, residency copy, ID card, salary certificate/trade licence, six months bank statements, copy of developer sale/ purchase agreement, downpayment receipt, cheque for loan processing fee.

Lender	Abu Dhabi Islamic Bank
Eligibility	UAE (Abu Dhabi) residents over 21 years old and under 70 years old with salary transferred to the bank.
Mortgage term	TBC
Interest rate	Variable
Maximum loan amount	AED 1.1 million
Insurance requirement	TBC
Minimum salary	(AED) 8,000
Fees	AED 2,000
Eligible properties	All major developers, offplan properties and secondary market properties
Documentation	Application form, passport copy, ID card, six months bank statements, copy of developer sale/purchase agreement, land registry documents, valuation report, property plans, certificate of loan discharge from Loan Department.

Sharjah Islamic Bank offers Sharia compliant home loans to UAE and GCC nationals only, but may consider home loans to other nationalities on a case by case basis and subject to status.

The following banks offer mortgages to overseas investors in their own countries.

- ICICI Bank
- Bank Meli Iran
- Bank Saderat Iran
- National Bank of Oman
- Housing Bank For Trade & Finance

Abu Dhabi Commercial Bank
Tel: +971 2 6962222
Fax: +971 2 6450384
Website: www.adcb.com

Amlak Finance
Tel: +971 4 3673120
Fax: +971 4 3673121
Website: www.amlakfinance.com

Arab Bank
Tel: +971 4 2950845
Toll free: 800-27224
Fax: +971 4 2952596
Website: www.arabbak.ae

Barclays Bank
Tel: 800-22725297
Fax: +971 4 3663133
Website: www.barclays.ae

Dubai Islamic Bank
Tel: 8004766
Fax: +971 4 2954111
Website: www.dib.ae

Emirates Islamic Bank
Tel: +971 4 3160101
Fax: +971 4 2227321
Website: www.emiratesislamicbank.ae

Habib Bank AG Zurich
Tel: +971 4 3313999
Fax: +971 4 3317666
Website: www.habibbank.com

HSBC
Tel: +971 4 3434499
Toll Free: 800 5400
Fax: +971 4 3438586
Website: www.hsbc.ae

Lloyds TSB Bank
Tel: +971 4 3422000
Fax: +971 4 3422660
Website: www.lloydstsb.ae

Mashreq Bank
Tel: +971 4 2174800
Fax: +971 4 2148298
Website: www.mashreqbank.com

National Bank of Abu Dhabi
Tel: +971 4 2226141
Toll free: 800 2211
Fax: +971 4 2243777
Website: www.nbad.com

National Bank of Dubai
Tel: +971 4 2222111
Fax: +971 4 2283000
Website: www.nbd.com

RAK Bank
Tel: +971 4 2130978
Fax: +971 4 3370545
Website: www.rakbank.ae

Standard Chartered Bank
Tel: +971 4 3599550
Fax: +971 4 3526679
Website: www.standardchartered.com

Union National Bank
Tel: +971 4 2211188
Toll free: 800 2600
Fax: +971 4 2237440
Website: www.unb.com

Legal Advice

AL TAMIMI
& COMPANY

Advocates & Legal Consultants

التـــمـــيـــمــي
و مـــشــاركـــوه

للمحاماة والاستشارات القانونية

Al Tamimi & Company, originally established in 1989 by Essam Al Tamimi, is today one of the leading law firms in the Arabian Gulf region. It is the largest independent law firm in the United Arab Emirates with four offices in Dubai, Abu Dhabi, Sharjah and the Dubai Internet City. Clients are ably served by an international team of over 90 high-caliber lawyers from the United Kingdom, North America, Europe, South Africa, the United Arab Emirates and several other Arab countries. Each member of its team of professionals and qualified administrative staff is fully committed to providing clients with accurate, creative and cost effective advice. In addition, the firm has the largest and most experienced team of UAE national advocates with rights of audience before the UAE courts. This combination makes the firm unique in being able to offer clients first class representation in both consultancy and advocacy services.

The firm can assist multinational companies to establish operations in the UAE independently, or in association with local partners. Both local clients, many of whom have business interests outside the UAE, and international companies, rely on its global perspective. The firm subscribes to the belief that the world of opportunity does not recognise national boundaries.

Al Tamimi & Company specialises in:
Company / Commercial Law, Litigation, Banking / Securities, Project Finance, Islamic Finance, Construction Law, Insurance, Maritime Law, Aviation Law, Intellectual Property, Information Technology, E-Commerce, Mergers and Acquisitions, Joint Ventures, Alternative Dispute Resolution, Arbitration, Family Business and Property Law.

Al Tamimi & Company is also the most subscribed source of legal information in the region. The firm publishes a monthly newsletter covering the GCC and Middle East region called 'Law Update'. The firm is highly regarded for its opinion on the local legal perspective and is poised to offer clients advice and counsel regarding all regional business operations and concerns.

Foreign Ownership of Property in the United Arab Emirates

Introduction
In the absence of a federal law regulating foreign ownership of property in the United Arab Emirates, this article examines the legal status and common practices in the individual emirates to discover the availability of foreign ownership of property generally throughout the United Arab Emirates. Undoubtedly, foreign ownership of property has a sovereign and political impact and the United Arab Emirates is handling this very carefully, due to the nature of the demographic map of the country, as well as other economic considerations.

Until recently, foreigners have effectively been prevented from registering ownership of property in the United Arab Emirates pursuant to common practice, but without any legislation applied on a federal level to this effect. In fact, the Civil Code is generally silent on the matter, but local decisions were issued, i.e. that issued by the Emirate of Abu Dhabi, which prohibited nationals and non-nationals from disposing of land through sale or purchase, or any other forms of disposal, except for inheritance and grants. The Civil Procedures Code (Federal Law No. (11) of 1992) states in Article (298) that selling of property shall be prohibited except for sale to a UAE National; but this statement is made under Chapter Six relating to attachment and sale of property and therefore, the text of Article (298) should not be applied beyond this. As mentioned above, the Civil Code is silent on any express prohibition against foreign ownership. As a result of the development boom throughout the UAE and the colossal achievements of the real estate sector and its contribution to the national economy, the general policy is now changing in relation to foreign ownership and is leaning towards greater flexibility in this regard, which is evident in the local laws passed recently by some of the emirates. We can summarize the current legal status and common practices in the various emirates in relation to foreign ownership of property as follows:

Dubai

Pursuant to Law No. (7) of 2006 in connection with the registration of real property in the Emirate of Dubai, UAE and GCC nationals and companies wholly owned by them have the right to own any property in Dubai and to seek registration of title at the Dubai Lands Department. Further, the Dubai Lands Department will register a number of property rights including a freehold interest, a long term lease of up to 99 years, a usufruct right and a right of musataha (ground development). The law also grants foreigners the right to own a freehold interest, a long term lease of up to 99 years or a usufruct right in specific designated areas in Dubai as determined by the Ruler's approval. The first of such approvals came by way of Regulation No. (3) of 2006 wherein the Ruler of Dubai designated 23 areas for foreign ownership. Law No. (8) of 2007 concerning the establishment of escrow accounts for real estate development projects in Dubai was recently enacted. Essentially a consumer protection law, the law regulates real estate developers' receipt and use of instalment payments from purchasers in connection with the sale of off plan properties. The law also requires developers to register with the Lands Department prior to engaging in development activities. Finally, it is anticipated that the Strata Law will be issued in the near future, which law will likely govern the creation, registration and management of jointly owned property in Dubai. The law will also presumably establish the rights and obligations of individual unit owners with regards to voting rights in their homeowners association, the payment of service charges and their relative ownership in the common areas.

Abu Dhabi

According to Law No. (19) of 2005 with regards to property ownership, the right to own property in Abu Dhabi is restricted to UAE nationals and legal entities wholly owned by them. An exception to this rule, however, grants GCC nationals the right to own property within certain designated "Investment Areas". The law also grants foreigners the right to own apartments or floors within a building (without the right of ownership of the underlying land) in the Investment Areas, together with the right to own a 99 year lease and a right of Musataha (ground development) for a period of 50 years, renewable upon the mutual consent of the parties. At present, the only Investment Areas that have been officially declared are Al Reem Island and Al Raha Beach although it is expected that further areas will be designated Investment Area status. Law No. (19) of 2005 was later amended by Law No. 2 of 2007, which law grants Abu Dhabi's Executive Council the authority to grant any person or company the right to own property anywhere in the Emirate of Abu Dhabi regardless of the location or nationality of such party. In essence, this provision allows the Executive Council to make exceptions in special cases to allow GCC and foreign nationals the right to own property in areas of Abu Dhabi which fall outside the Investment Zones.

Sharjah

Decision No. (32) of 2005 provides that UAE and GCC nationals are permitted to own property in all areas of Sharjah. All other nationalities are not generally permitted to own property, but the Ruler's approval may be obtained in special circumstances. Through observation of current common practice in the Emirate, foreigners can lease property and register their leases with the Sharjah Lands Department so long as the term of the lease is for a maximum of five years.

Ajman

The Emirate of Ajman is considered to be the most liberal among the Emirates in relation to foreign ownership of property. That being said, there are presently no laws granting property rights to foreigners. An Amiri Decree may be issued to a foreigner requesting the right to own property in Ajman. Restrictions apply, however, as there are certain areas in the Emirate where non UAE nationals are historically not permitted to own property. The grant of a long term lease to foreigners is not prohibited according to Amiri Decree No (6) of 2005 regarding the Regulation of Real Estate Leasing in the Emirate of Ajman. It is anticipated that a set of laws relating to the real estate sector and foreign ownership will be issued, as they are currently under consideration by the Executive Council in the Emirate.

Fujairah

Fujairah has the disadvantage of a shortage of land that can be developed, since two thirds of the land in this Emirate is mountainous and too rugged for development. Fujairah does not currently allow foreign ownership of property, and this extends to GCC nationals unless they obtain an Amiri Decree allowing them to own property. The Emirate is becoming very popular, however, with a swathe of developments particularly along the coast. There are currently some projects being undertaken by private companies in association with the government of Fujairah, which are expected to grant a right of foreign ownership of property, and there are currently ongoing discussions to grant 99 leases to foreigners in this respect. As there is currently no local law which regulates the relationship between landlords and tenants in Fujairah, the grant of long term leases to foreigners with a term of 99 years would be permissible.

Ras Al Khaimah

According to Decision No. (20) of 2005, UAE nationals can own property in all areas of Ras Al Khaimah. GCC nationals are not specifically provided for in this Decision, but it is understood that they will be treated the same as UAE nationals. All other nationalities can own property in specific investment projects by establishing a company in the Ras Al Khaimah Free Zone. In 2003, a law regulating flat ownership in Ras Al Khaimah was issued, which law granted the right of ownership of apartments in Ras Al Khaimah. The law also has provisions relating to co-owners' associations and grants pre-emption rights to unit owners within the same building. The law is silent, however, as to whether foreigners can purchase flats in Ras Al Khaimah. Decision No. (18) of 2005 granted the Ras Al-Khaimah Real Estate Company PJSC certain lands for the development of a variety of commercial and residential real estate projects. This law is also silent as to foreign ownership, but the law has been interpreted as authorizing foreign ownership of the residential and commercial units developed by the Ras Al-Khaimah Real Estate Company PJSC.

Umm Al Quwain

Pursuant to Law No. (3) of 2006, UAE nationals, GCC nationals, corporate entities wholly owned by them and public joint stock companies have the right to own property anywhere within the Emirate. Foreigners have the right to own multi-storey developments (excluding the underlying land itself) in designated "Investment Zones". Foreigners may also possess a usufruct right for a period not to exceed 99 years and a musataha right for a period of fifty years (renewable upon the mutual consent of the parties) within the Investment Zones. Through observation of current common practice in the Emirate, any company with foreign partners can own real estate by obtaining an Amiri Decree.

Al Tamimi & Company

PO Box 9275

Dubai International Financial Centre

6th Floor, Building 4 East

Dubai

United Arab Emirates

Tel: +971 4 3641641

Fax: +971 4 3641777

Email: marketing@tamimi.com

Website: www.tamimi.com

BSA

BSA was founded by Dr Rashid Bin Shabib in 2001 and is today a dynamic law firm whose character has been shaped through the adaptive innovation of its talented lawyers. BSA's reputation is built through the successful synergy of personable and approachable professionals with quality clients and through strong relationships with key local and regional authorities.

In recent years BSA's growth has been achieved through assembling a team of innovative legal minds with quality UAE experience who are supported by BSA's affiliates in the GCC & MENA region, Europe and America. True to its pioneering nature, BSA was the first UAE based law firm to be licensed by the Dubai International Financial Centre.

In the UAE's progressive and fast-developing business environment, clients seeking legal guidance and support enjoy the privilege of accessing BSA's adaptive and innovative legal intelligence.

BSA was the first UAE-based law firm to register with the Dubai International Financial Centre (DIFC) and has an established track record of operating with transparency and providing high quality and cost efficient legal services.

Recent legal developments in the real estate sector and their effects on various aspects of the industry – An overview

By Jimmy Haoula, Managing Partner

Over the last few years we have witnessed some dramatic legal developments in the real estate sector in Dubai. One of the turning points was the introduction of the Real Estate Law No 7 of 2006 which has had a multi-fold effect on the many significant aspects operating within the industry. The new laws aim to define the parameters and regulate the real estate sector setting industry standards for developers, lenders, investors, agents and the authorities.

Mortgages

A mortgage is a loan to purchase a real estate property, usually with pre-determined payment periods and interest rates, and involves the transfer of interest in a property as security for a loan. Mortgage firms give the mortgagee a lien on the property as collateral for the loan.

Mortgages are the most common method of financing real estate transactions in the UAE in general and the Emirate of Dubai in particular.

Article 24(2) of the Real Estate Law No 7 of 2006 issued on 13 March 2006 states as follows:

"In the Land Unit record shall be set out any conditions, promises or restrictions concerning Rights over Land and other obligations".

As per the above article, it is required to register a real estate mortgage with the Dubai Land Department (DLD).

In the relation of the mortgagor/ mortgagee, the mortgagee will be requested by the mortgagor to make monthly installments for a specific period of time which includes the amount borrowed as well as the interest on the principal amount.

Failure to make payments results in the foreclosure of the mortgage. The most common foreclosure processes are court proceedings (judicial foreclosure) or grants of power to the mortgagee to sell the property both of which are standard provisions in any mortgage agreement entered by the mortgagee and the mortgagor.

Is it possible to get a mortgage for a real estate property in Dubai?
Yes, as per Article 24 of the Law, non GCC nationals are allowed to register mortgages over their properties with the DLD. The DLD charges 0.25% of the value of the borrowed amount.

Due to the considerable boost in the mortgage sector caused essentially by the implementation of the Law, various local and international financial institutions are now investing in financing real estate.

How does a standard mortgage differ from an Islamic mortgage?
Islamic finance is "the provision of financial services on a basis that is compliant with the principles and rules of Islamic commercial jurisprudence (fiqh al mu'amalat), a branch of Islamic Shari'ah jurisprudence."

There are three key differences between a standard mortgage and an Islamic mortgage and can be defined as follows:

The no-interest rule - the mortgagor cannot earn interest on the loan nor is the mortgagee required to pay interest. No interest charges are applied in Islamic mortgage however the beneficiary from the Islamic mortgage will be asked by the financial institution from which he borrowed the loan to pay a fee or profit, or both over time.

The prohibition of illegality - Islamic instruments invest only in worthy and eligible causes from an Islamic perspective.

The prohibition of uncertainty - the subject of a contract must not be prohibited under Shari'ah. If a contract offends the religious or moral principles of Islam, it becomes illegal and unenforceable.

What are the mortgage rates in Dubai?
Mortgage rates offered in the market vary between 6% to 8% and are considered expensive when compared to similar rates in other countries.

How do local finance firms assess mortgage applications?
In the Dubai market the mortgage lenders not only assess the application in light of the asset and its performance with time but also consider the applicant, his/her monthly income and expenses. Therefore we always advise people to check the possibility of obtaining a mortgage and the amount that they are eligible to borrow before finalizing any sale and purchase of a property.

What documents are required by mortgage firms to obtain finance?
Most of the financing firms have the following standard requirements:
1. Proof of residency
2. Income details of the applicant
3. Letter of employment (for employed applicants) or proof of partnership i.e. copy of the Memorandum of Association and license for the company (for investors)
4. Six months' bank statements (for employed applicants) or three years' audited accounts (for self-employed applicants).

Since the declaration of Dubai Law No.7 of 2006, concerning Real Property registration in the Emirate of Dubai many investors and purchasers were attracted and encouraged by one way or another to purchase a property in Dubai. This Law authorizes all foreigners to own freehold titles in the city within the specific areas determined by the Ruler of the Emirate. However, most property purchasers and investors have serious concerns about the applicable law to their wills and inheritance in the UAE.

In general, inheritance and wills in the UAE are regulated by the UAE Civil Code, Federal Law No.2 of 1987 (the "Code") and the Personal Affairs Law No.28 of 2005 (the "Law"). Whilst it is not entirely clear, it would seem that the law of a foreigner (the law of his own country) will be the applicable law on his inheritance and will, in case he passed away. This can be observed from Article 17/1 of the Code which provides that "Inheritance shall be governed by the law of the deceased at the time of his death".

In addition, the Code stresses that the form of wills and the substantive provisions governing testamentary disposition and other dispositions taking affect after death shall be governed by the law of:

1. The state of which the person making such dispositions is a national at the time of his death;
2. The state of which the person making such disposition is a national at the time the disposition is made, or
3. The state in which the disposition is made (Article 17/3 and 17/4 of the Code).

However, the UAE lawmaker has made remarkable exceptions and restrictions to the above. These exceptions demand the full attention and consideration of all foreign property purchasers.

Firstly, property rights located in the UAE which belong to a foreigner having no heir shall become vested in the UAE.

Secondly, the Laws of the UAE are the applicable laws to wills made by foreigners disposing their real property located in the UAE (Article 17/5).

Thirdly, matters relating to personal status such as marriage, inheritance, and lineage, and matters relating to sovereignty, freedom of trade, the circulation of wealth, rules of private ownership and the other rules and foundations upon which society is based, in such manner as not to conflict with the definitive provisions and fundamental principles of the Islamic Shari'ah are all deemed to be Rules of the Public order (Article 3 of the Code). Therefore, in spite of what have been said above, it is not permissible in the UAE to apply the provisions of a law specified by article 17 of the Code (the Law of the deceased), if such provisions are contrary to rules of public order or morals of the UAE (Article 27 of the Code).

In other words, no matter what the religion or nationality of the deceased and whether he has a will or not, his inheritance and will, will only be distributed and enforced in accordance with the laws of the country of which the deceased is a national at the time of his death to an extent that it does not contradict with the UAE public order.

This gray area was partially clarified by Dubai cassation Court in 1998 when it ruled that the differences of the fixed shares of the heirs between the local laws and the laws of the state of which the deceased is a national shall not be considered as public order.

These issues are very critical. Unfortunately most international investors and property purchasers are not aware of them. Therefore, consulting a lawyer about the risks associated with such investments can save a great deal of time, money and unnecessary inconvenience.

Escrow Account Law

The Law No 8 of 2007, also known as Trust Account Law or Escrow Account Law, was passed on 3rd June 2007. Although the law came into immediate effect, real estate developers in Dubai have a grace period of 6 months from the date of publication of the law in the official gazette to adjust their status in accordance with the provisions of this law.

What is the new concept introduced by the law?
The law has created a new escrow scheme to be applied for the sale of off-plan property developments in Dubai. For the purpose of this Law, off-plan units refer to partitioned parts of a property development under construction.

The scheme involves:
- Depositing all payments made by purchasers to buy off-plan units in a specific bank account; and
- Operating this bank account in accordance with the pre-determined terms and conditions approved by the Dubai Land Department (DLD).

In this scheme, the DLD shall be the supervising body responsible for monitoring and locating any infringement of the provisions regulating the establishment and operation of the escrow account.

Is this Law applicable to all developers in Dubai?

Article 3 of the Law sets out that the provisions of this Law shall be applicable only to developers selling off-plan units and receiving payments from the purchasers prior to the completion of the real estate project.

What is the main purpose of this Law?

This new law comes as part of the on-going efforts made by the Dubai government to attract more purchasers to the real estate sector.

Prior to the enactment of the law some developers stalled the construction process causing massive delays which resulted in considerable damages to the purchasers. Also, until recently no restrictions or obligations were imposed on the developers to regulate their expenditures, however, now the new law gives certain guarantees and reassurances to purchasers making it a more feasible investment opportunity.

In addition, previously the purchasers faced the risk of foreign developers selling them off-plan units and then fleeing the country without completing the construction work. The law aims to address these concerns and to boost confidence in the real estate sector, however, more vigorous steps still need to be implemented.

What are the laws concerning advertisements of off-plans units?

As stated in Article 5 of the law, real estate developers cannot advertise in local or foreign media, or participate in local or foreign trade exhibitions to promote sale of units or properties under construction in Dubai unless they obtain a written approval from the DLD.

What are the requirements for the sale of off-plans units?

All developers wanting to sell off-plan units should be registered with the Registrar of Developers. In addition, they should obtain a special approval from the DLD for each individual real estate project.

For the purpose of obtaining special approval, the developer should provide the DLD with the following documents pertaining to each project:

i. Trade license;
ii. Dubai Chamber of Commerce & Industry Certificate;
iii. Title deed of the plot intended for the development;
iv. Copy of the agreement entered into between the master developer and the secondary developer;
v. Architectural designs and layouts approved by concerned authorities and the master developer;
vi. A balance sheet approved by an accredited legal auditor including a list of the expenses and the profits of the project;

vii. Undertaking signed by the master developer/secondary developer in which he covenants to start the construction work upon obtaining all the related approvals; and

viii. Copy of the sale and purchase agreement to be executed by the developer and the purchasers of the off-plan units.

What is the process for establishing an escrow account?

For each real estate project the developer should open a specific bank account at one of the accredited banks in the UAE. This bank account must be used solely for the purpose of that particular project.

The escrow account is established based on a written agreement between the escrow agent (the bank) and the developer, a copy of which must be deposited at the DLD. It is this agreement that regulates the operation of the account and specifies the rights and obligations of the parties.

It is worth mentioning that as per Article 9 the creditors of the developers are not entitled to seize any sums contained in the escrow account.

What is the process of operating the escrow account?

In accordance with Article 11 of the law, the escrow agent must regularly provide the DLD with statements specifying all amounts credited and debited from the escrow account.

Furthermore, the DLD can at any time request the escrow agent to provide documents it considers necessary for the assessment of the escrow account. Also, the DLD is entitled to appoint third parties in order to verify and audit such documents.

As per Article 12, the purchasers of the off-plan units are entitled at any time to review the bank statement pertaining to the escrow account.

Most importantly, Article 14 of the law states that on completion of the project the escrow agent must hold back 5 % of the total value of the trust account for a period of one year to meet any defects arising in the property during that period.

What are the punitive provisions under the Law?

If a real estate developer fails to register with the DLD and carries on with its activities, or provides false documentation for the purpose of obtaining a license, a fine of AED 100,000 and/or an imprisonment sanction will be inflicted on the breaching party.

Furthermore, a developer delaying the commencement of the construction work for over 6 months after obtaining the DLD approval, without any legitimate reason, will be de-registered.

A Legal Overview

The new law does not address a few important aspects affecting both developers and purchasers which hinder the progress of this sector.

Currently the licenses required to develop land, and sell and purchase property, are only granted to UAE or GCC nationals by the Dubai Economic Department (DED), hence foreign investors who have a title deed to a plot of land still need to go through local companies and contractors to get the appropriate licenses and the right to build developments on these plots which can act as a major deterrent to some developers entering the market.

Finally, although Article 17 of the law set out a time frame during which the developer must start the construction work in order to avoid de-registration, there are still no restrictions provided in this law to prevent extensive delays in the completion which can inflict severe damages on the investors.

Constitution of RERA

On 31 July 2007, H.H Sheikh Mohammed bin Rashid Al Maktoum, Vice President of the UAE and Ruler of Dubai, issued a decree establishing the Real Estate Regulatory Authority (RERA) in Dubai.

According to the decree, the jurisdiction of RERA will mainly cover the following:

- Issuing real-estate policies, strategies and regulations;
- Registering real estate agents, brokers and developers; and
- Conducting studies related to the real estate sector

RERA will be overseeing the operations of property developers, management companies, financing institutions, brokers and owners' associations.

Over the past five years Dubai has emerged as one of the fastest growing cities in the world boasting of the tallest building, soon the biggest mall and the most ambitious land reclamation projects ever undertaken. This immense expansion in construction must be supplemented by the creation of modern rules, legislations and formation of new authorities to help ensure long term stability in the real estate and property sector in Dubai.

Up until now, real estate matters were dealt with strictly by the Dubai Land Department (DLD), the Rent Committee at the Dubai Municipality, and the Dubai Department of Economic Development. However, with the constitution of RERA, the control over all essential real estate activities will now be transferred to this new regulatory body.

RERA's powers in relation to existing authorities:

- All companies applying to carry out real estate related activities in Dubai will need to get an approval from RERA prior to submitting their application to the Dubai Department of Economic Development.

- RERA will also be in charge of registering real estate brokers and agents in addition to circulating template contracts regulating the standard terms of agreements between real estate agents and third party investors.

- RERA will be preparing standard templates of lease agreements and will be forming a new tribunal in charge of resolving disputes between landlords and tenants. This tribunal will replace the Dubai Rent Committee.

RERA is set to become the most influential authority within the real estate sector in the UAE.

RERA's powers vis-à-vis recently introduced laws:

- Regarding the latest Trust Account Law, every developer will be required to obtain the approval of RERA prior to setting up a trust account at one of the approved banks.

- RERA will be involved in applying the new Strata Law expected to be issued shortly. The Strata Law will regulate the management of communal areas in common hold properties, which refers to lifts, swimming pools, corridors, car parking spaces, etc. The final draft of the law has been approved however it is not signed yet.

- RERA will also be taking charge of rental issues with regard to a new law regulating the relationship between landlords and tenants. A first draft of the law has been issued and waiting for final approval. The expected law will set the major rules for leasing commercial and residential properties and given that the rental rates in Dubai are among the highest in the world, having an authority like RERA will help organize and regulate most rental issues, whilst giving consumers the assurance that their rights will be better protected.

- RERA will also work on the planning and development of the real estate and property sector involving the calculation of statistics. This information will be accessible online through RERA's official website which will be launched shortly.

The industry is evolving at a very fast pace with new decrees and amendments coming into effect on regular basis. This definitely is a positive step towards regulating one of the most prominent industry sectors of Dubai. Although the challenges for achieving this have been significant, fortunately, the ongoing efforts promise even better results.

Contributed by: Bin Shabib & Associates (BSA) LLP Advocates & Legal Consultants, Level 6 East Wing Building 3, The Gate Precinct, Dubai International Financial Centre (DICF) PO Box 262 Dubai, United Arab Emirates Tel: +9714 368 5555 Fax: +9714 368 5000 info@bsa.ae www.bsa.ae

Trench & associates
LEGAL CONSULTANCY

Trench & Associates is a legal consultancy firm founded by Ms. Cynthia Trench in 1996. We combine a range of legal disciplines and are known as leaders in our areas of specialization, namely Corporate & Commercial Law, Property, Litigation and Intellectual Property Law.

Our Corporate and Commercial Department specialises in establishment of businesses. We offer a complete package designed to provide an efficient service with the least disruption to our Clients.

Our Litigation Department is comprised of experienced lawyers specialising in local and international Commercial, Corporate and Civil Litigation. We have strong associations with local advocates and have also developed litigation strategies for our Clients in various other countries.

Our new Property Department assists Clients in respect of sale and/or purchase of properties, vetting Developers' Agreements, advising clients on tenancy issues and disputes as well as a plethora of issues arising from Property transactions.

General Inquiry Email: coordinator@trenchlaw.com
Website: www.trenchlaw.com

HELENE MATHIEU Legal Consultants

Founded by Hélène Mathieu, a Canadian Barrister and Solicitor, **HELENE MATHIEU Legal Consultants** is a multilingual* team of experienced attorneys and consultants with a shared vision of distinction.

We do not presume to be the biggest, but we are committed to delivering the very best results based on our policy of straightforward communication and exclusive client care. Supported by an internal Advanced IT Knowledge Management System we have instant access to dynamic information with a vital impact on our clients' business.

- Real Estate. Private and corporate purchase, due diligence and legal representation
- Business Set-up and Start-up in the UAE
- Incorporation of offshore companies
- Set-up in Free Zones relevant to business activity
- Notary and Attestation services
- Legal document drafting, review and translation
- Labor disputes
- Family law
- Wills and Successions
- Legal services for Canadians in the UAE
- Immigration to Canada

* English, French, Arabic, Russian, German, Spanish, Hindi, Malayalam, and Tagalog

New Escrow Law

The unprecedented increase in expatriate population in the United Arab Emirates, scaling-up tourist numbers and the array of existing and upcoming international projects have resulted in a burgeoning property boom in Dubai on a mind-boggling scale, which roots can be traced back to 2002 when the Ruler of Dubai His Highness Sheikh Mohammed bin Rashid Al Maktoum announced that freehold ownership of certain properties in the Emirate was available to investors of all nationalities.

Although the property market in Dubai has grown tremendously, the legal framework has not developed at the same pace. In land law terms, the UAE is a new and developing jurisdiction and quite an array of relevant real estate answers concerning the rights of foreign property owners is simply not yet available. However, in its strife to build an internationally recognized and reliable property market, the Government of Dubai is taking steps to develop comprehensive land laws. After passing the Land Law for the Emirate, Dubai authorities introduced further legislation in July 2007 to protect real estate purchasers, especially those who are buying properties "off-plan" and are being asked to pay large down payments to the developer before the property is physically built.

Indeed, thousands of purchasers have paid a large percentage of the purchase price to developers or sub-developers of the property prior to receiving transfer of ownership. In most cases their properties are still under construction and hand-over is scheduled for some time in the future. Where is the guarantee that the planned and half-purchased property will be delivered, with the money at the entire disposal of the developer? The recently passed Escrow Law, or Law on Guarantee Accounts, safeguards the interests of such property purchasers, especially freehold buyers.

Critical to protecting consumers and ensuring the viability of the Dubai real estate industry, Escrow Law is a standard mechanism that has been used in other markets for many years. For example, in the USA or South Africa the purchaser of the property entrusts the purchase price to a lawyer, to be kept for the benefit of the developer in a special "Trust Account", until such time as either a certificate is issued that the building is completed; or the property is registered in the name of the purchaser; or the transaction is cancelled and the purchase price is dealt with accordingly.

So what exactly is Escrow? An Escrow is the deposit of funds with a neutral third party (the Escrow Agent). The Escrow Agent is given specific instructions as to how and when the funds may be paid out. An Escrow is therefore a legal arrangement to assist parties to perform their contracts and avoid disagreements. The Escrow Agent holds the Escrow deposit until it can be released to the Beneficiary upon the happening of some future event, or the performance of certain contractual conditions.

How the concept of an Escrow is addressed in the recent Law No. (8) Concerning Guarantee Accounts of Real Estate Development in the Emirate of Dubai is explained below.

The law applies to uncompleted off-plan property developments in the Emirate of Dubai and relates to both master and sub-developers.

Article (6) of Chapter (2) stipulates that from now onwards developers of new residential or commercial real estate projects will have to apply to the Dubai Land Department to open a guarantee account ("trust" or "escrow account").

To do so, developers will have to submit certain documents, including the title deed of the plot under development, a letter of approval from the master developer, approved architectural designs and layouts, approved balance sheet on payable installments, a copy of a sale contract to take place between the developer and the future buyers, along with the trade license and building permit. If all these documents are in order, the guarantee bank account will be opened under the name of the property being developed, based on the provisions of a written agreement between the developer and the Land Department.

All the down payments and installments made by the buyers of the property units will be deposited in the guarantee account. Both the buyers and the developer or their representatives have the right to examine the records of the account at any time.

What happens to the deposits next will be governed by a guarantee account manager. The account manager will audit the account and release payments to the developer according to the conditions of the sale contract. Prior to the release of any payment, the account manager will request a certificate from the developer issued by the engineering consultant of the development stating that a certain construction stage has been reached and that the next stage is in progress. Upon the receipt of such certificate, the guarantee account manager will inform the Land Department of the intention to release a payment to the developer.

The Dubai Escrow Law imposes fines of no less than AED 200,000 for the violation of any of the provisions of the law and insures maximum protection for property buyers even after the development is completed. The Land Department will keep 5 per cent of the project value in the guarantee account for one year after completion until all units of the property and title deeds are registered in the names of buyers.

The new Law No. 8 will help ensure that the buyers' down payments and installments are safeguarded in the government-approved banks and will add security to the real estate development to the thriving market of the Emirate. Property purchasers can now rest assured: Their real estate investments in Dubai are safe and will be used correctly under governmental supervision.

Helene Mathieu Legal Consultants
P.O. Box 28845, Dubai
United Arab Emirates

Tel: +971 4 3525303
Fax: +971 4 3519877
Email: info@hmlc.ae
Website: www.hmlc.ae

CLYDE&CO كلايدو مشاركوه

Clyde & Co

Clyde & Co is the leading full-service commercial law firm in the Gulf. It also has the largest presence in the region of any international law firm. Clyde & Co has offices in Dubai, Abu Dhabi and Qatar and has carried out work extensively throughout the AGCC states and the wider Middle East region. Clyde & Co also operates an Indian subcontinent practice from its offices in Dubai. For Clyde & Co's clients it's a winning combination. With over 90 lawyers and paralegals across 3 GCC offices they offer a unique range of international commercial and legal experience, cultural knowledge and depth of specialisation.

The property team in the Middle East offers a fully comprehensive service working with clients both in the UAE and internationally. A wide ranging expertise spans investment, development, funding, retail, leisure, mixed use, landlord and tenant and environment related transactions and the available resource enables the firm to handle projects of any size.

> ## An Introduction to Inheritance Law in the United Arab Emirates for Non-Resident Property Owners

Which Inheritance Laws Apply

The United Arab Emirates (the "UAE") is a federation of seven emirates comprising Abu Dhabi, Dubai, Ajman, Fujairah, Sharjah, Ras Al Khaimah and Umm Al Quwain. Matters of inheritance are governed principally by two federal laws, Federal Law No. 5 of 1985 regarding the law of Civil Transactions in the UAE (the "Civil Code") and Federal Law No. 28 of 2005 regarding the UAE Personal Affairs Law (the "Personal Affairs Law"). Federal laws apply to all emirates and are founded on the principles of Sharia, a system of devising Islamic law based on the Quran. The inheritance laws draw a distinction between Muslim UAE nationals and non Muslim, non-UAE nationals and determine whether or not Sharia will apply to a deceased's estate.

The general rule in the UAE is that inheritance issues for Muslim UAE nationals will be dealt with in accordance with Sharia and for foreigners, the law of the deceased's home country will apply. It is not clear, however, whether this general rule applies to real estate located in the UAE. Whereas the Civil Code states in one part that the law of the home country will apply to matters of inheritance, it later states that where a Will made by a foreigner deals with the disposal of real estate in the UAE, UAE law will apply.

Real Property Rights under the Civil Code

Real property rights under the Civil Code are governed by the principle of lex situs i.e the law of the state where the property is located shall apply. It was hoped that the Personal Affairs Law would add clarity to the terms of the Civil Code and whilst it does confirm that the laws of an expatriate's home country would apply to matters of inheritance for foreigners, it makes no specific reference to real estate located in the UAE. Opinion is divided as to whether or not the general provisions of the Personal Affairs Law override the specific restrictions of the Civil Code. Some believe that if a non-UAE national makes a specific reference in their Will to the disposal of property in the UAE, a Court will follow the wishes of the deceased. Others believe that the Personal Affairs Law only applies to general matters of inheritance and that the inheritance of real property will continue to be governed by the Civil Code. Ultimately, it is up to the UAE Courts to decide which laws to apply on a case by case basis.

If the Court decides to apply local law, or if the law of the deceased's home country states that local law should apply to matters of inheritance, the provisions of Sharia will apply. A Sharia scholar must be appointed to identify the heirs of the deceased and to determine the fixed share of the estate that each heir will receive.

Cases in the UAE are initially heard by the Court of First Instance and can be appealed at the Court of Appeal and then finally at the Court of Cassation. Court proceedings in the UAE can be lengthy and expensive. All issues of inheritance for foreigners will first be heard at the Court of First Instance.

Offshore Company as Purchasing Vehicle

One way individuals have tried to avoid the application of UAE law to the disposal of property, is to incorporate an offshore company to purchase/own the property. If the property is owned in the company's name, ownership of the property can be transferred by transferring shares in the company. Therefore, if a shareholder dies, it is their shares that will be disposed of and not the real property itself. This would appear to avoid the specific provision in the Civil Code that matters of real estate must be dealt with in accordance with the UAE law and means that the general provision allowing the laws of the home country to apply to general matters of inheritance will be followed. There are however, potential disadvantages to this approach. In particular, many banks are reluctant to offer mortgage finance and checking facilities to offshore companies, and there are time and cost implications when incorporating an offshore company. The reference to 'off-shore' here also does not include Jebel Ali Free Zone or Ras Al Khaimah Free Zone offshore companies. It is risky to use these types of offshore companies to specifically avoid the application of Sharia law, as share transfers must be registered with the relevant free zone authority, and if they are aware of the death, the transfer may be rejected or invalidated without a Court Order.

A "Reserved Portion" applies under Sharia Law

Under Sharia law each heir has a 'reserved portion' of the estate that will be distributed to him or her. The guidelines surrounding how these reserved portions are calculated are complex and in each case a Sharia scholar will be appointed to decide how the estate is distributed. As a general example, if a father leaves behind a wife, a son and a daughter, the wife would receive one eighth or less of the total estate, of the remainder the son would receive up to two thirds and the daughter would receive up to one third.

Under Sharia law all illegitimate or adopted children are excluded from being heirs and if an heir is still in utero at the time of death, the estate cannot be distributed until it is born because the fixed shares of the estate will depend on whether the heir is male or female.

According to the Civil Code, if a foreigner has no heirs, then any real property owned by them and located in the UAE will become vested in the state.

The need to make a Will

Generally, Muslims do not make a Will because the principles of Sharia will automatically apply to their inheritance.

As discussed above, there remains some uncertainty with the law surrounding inheritance for UAE real estate owned by foreigners, and for this reason it is advisable to make a Will to clarify a deceased's wishes regarding the disposal of his estate. It is not necessary to make a local Will because the Courts will look at whether the Will is valid in the country of origin. It would appear best practice for individuals who own property in the UAE, but do not live in the UAE, to have their Will attested by the UAE Embassy in their home country. All of this makes it easier for the Court to determine whether there is a valid Will and if the deceased has opted for the laws of their home country to apply.

Where there is no Will it will be up to the local Courts to decide whether the property is disposed of in accordance with local or home country law.

No restrictions on making gifts before death

According to Sharia law anything owned by the deceased at the time of his death (excluding stolen items, items acquired by breach of trust and government or employer pensions) is considered part of his estate. No restrictions apply on making gifts before the death. However, the beneficiary of the gift must be in actual possession of the gift upon the death of the donor otherwise it will be considered owned by the donor at the time of his death and therefore part of his estate.

Guardianship

Under the provisions of the Personal Affairs Law, a guardian must be appointed to receive property left to a child or person without full legal capacity. Once the child reaches eighteen years of age the guardian may permit him to receive or manage some or all of the property. The guardianship is first awarded to the father, then to a male heir on the father's side in accordance with the order of inheritance.

Importance of Property Registration

The UAE courts will look at the evidence of ownership to determine who actually owns the property and it is therefore important for property owners to register their ownership at the local

Land Department if possible. There is no equivalent to the "right of survivorship" concept found in other jurisdictions (i.e. where property passes to the surviving joint owner on death of a joint owner). The presumption in the UAE is that joint owners will hold the property in equal shares unless stipulated otherwise.

For further information, please contact
Alexis Waller or Catherine Gill
Clyde & Co
Dubai Office: PO Box 7001
Suite 102, City Tower 2
Sheikh Zayed Road
Dubai
United Arab Emirates

Tel: +971 4 3311102
Fax: +971 4 3319920
Website: www.clydeco.com

Anders Legal Consultancy
Tel: +971 4 3356983
Fax: +971 4 3356986
Website: www.anders.ae

Al Dhaheri International, Advocates & Legal
Consultants
Tel: +971 4 2682822
Fax: +971 4 2682820
Website: www.dubailegaleagle.com

Al Jabri Law Firm
Tel: +971 2 6269050
Fax: +971 2 6269040
Website: www.aljabrilegal.com

AL Jazeera Advocates & Legal Consultants
Tel: +971 4 2666363
Fax: +971 4 2662206
Email: aliazadv@emirates.net.ae

Al Khaleej Advocates & Legal Consultants
Tel: +971 4 2288808
Fax: +971 4 2288863
Website: www.uaeattorneys.com

Al Kumity Advocates
Tel: +971 4 2686855
Fax: + 971 4 2622959
Website: www.alkumity.com

Al Midfa & Associates
Tel: +971 4 2272701
Fax: +971 4 2277422
Website: www.almidfalawyers.com

Al Tamimi & Company Advocates & Legal
Consultants
Tel: +971 4 3641641
Fax: +971 4 3641777
Website: www.tamimi.com

Bin Shabib & Assocaites (BSA) LLP
Tel: +971 4 3685555
Fax: +971 4 3685000
Website: www.bsa.ae

Clyde & Co
Tel: +971 4 3311102
Fax: +971 4 3319920
Website: www.clydeco.com

Denton Wilde Sapte
Tel: +971 4 3310220
Fax: +971 4 3310201
Website: www.dentonwildesapte.com

Dr Ibrahim Al Mulla
Tel: +971 2 6277725
Fax: +971 2 6277708
Website: www.dralmulla.com

Emirates International Law Firm
Tel: +971 2 6265600
Fax: +971 2 6265123
Website: www.eilf.com

Hadef Al Dhahiri & Associates
Tel: +971 4 3323222
Fax: +971 4 3323300
Website: www.hadalaw.com

Hadler & Partner Legal Consultants
Tel: +971 2 6219050
Fax: +971 2 6219030
Website: www.hadlerpartner.com

Helene Mathieu Legal Consultants
Tel: +971 4 3525303
Fax: +971 4 3519877
Website: www.hmlc.ae

Hikmat Fayad & Associates
Tel: +971 4 2222888
Fax: +971 4 2274870

Hugh Fraser International Legal Consultants
Tel: +971 4 3320007
Fax: +971 4 3320008
Website: www.fraserlegal.com

KAS Legal
Tel: +941 4 3347447
Fax: +971 4 3350644
Website: www.kaslaws.com

Key & Dixon
Tel: +971 4 3323324
Fax: +971 4 3323325
Website: www.keydixon.com

Legal Maxims
Tel: +971 4 2298222
Fax: +971 4 2211125
Website: www.legalmaxims.com

Maamoun Al Khouli & Associates
Tel: +971 504538887
Website: www.alkhouli.ae

Meyer Reumann Legal Consultancy
Tel: +971 4 3317110
Fax: +971 4 3313832
Website: www.meyer-reumann.com

Nasser Malalla Advocates & Legal Consultants
Tel: +971 4 2833341
Fax: +971 4 2833347

NJQ & Assocaites
Tel: +971 4 2722175
Fax: +971 4 2722574
Website: www.qumsieh.com

Rashid Bin Arab Office Advocates & Legal Consultants
Tel: +971 6 5750999
Fax: +971 6 5750777

Reed Smith Richards Butler
Tel: +971 2 6222636
Fax: +971 2 6222625
Website: www.reedsmith.com

Rouse & Co. International Ltd.
Tel: +971 4 2247678
Fax: +971 4 2247658
Website: www.iprights.com

Simmons & Simmons
Tel: +971 2 6275568
Fax: +971 2 6275223
Website: www.simmons-simmons.com

Trench & Associates
Tel: +971 4 3553146
Fax: +971 4 3553106
Website: www.trenchlaw.com

Notes

Notes